Toronto Between the Wars

Toronto Between the Wars

Life in the City 1919-1939

CHARIS COTTER

FIREFLY BOOKS

A FIREFLY BOOK

Published by Firefly Books Ltd. 2004

First printing

NATIONAL LIBRARY OF CANADA CATALOGUING IN PUBLICATION DATA
Cotter, Charis
      Toronto between the wars : life in the city 1919-1939 / Charis Cotter.

Includes bibliographical references and index.
ISBN 1-55297-899-0

      1. Toronto (Ont.)—History—20th century. I. Title.

FC3097.4.C673 2004   971.3'54103   C2004-900993-1

PUBLISHER CATALOGING-IN-PUBLICATION DATA (U.S.)
Cotter, Charis.
      Toronto between the wars : life in the city 1919–1939 / Charis Cotter. _1st ed.
[224] p. : photos. ;   cm.
Includes bibliographical references and index.
Summary: Photographs and text capture the changing face of Toronto, Ontario, between the two world wars.
ISBN 1-55297-899-0 (pbk.)
1. Toronto (Ont.)—History—20th century — Pictorial works. I. Title.
971.3541/ 0222 dc22   F1059.5.T6843.C688 2004

Published in Canada in 2004 by
Firefly Books Ltd.
66 Leek Crescent
Richmond Hill, Ontario L4B 1H1

Published in the United States in 2004 by
Firefly Books (U.S.) Inc.
P.O. Box 1338, Ellicott Station
Buffalo, New York 14205

Designed by Bob Wilcox
Printed in Canada by Friesens, Altona, Manitoba

The Publisher acknowledges the financial support of the Government of Canada through the Book Publishing Industry Development Program for its publishing activities.

FRONT COVER: **Looking north from Queen and Yonge streets, April 1938.**
FRONT FLAP: **Filming the Toronto skyline from a northern vantage point, late 1920s.**
PAGE 2: **Grenadier Pond, High Park, 1923.**
PAGE 7: **A child mails a letter, November 1925.**
BACK COVER (TOP): **Selling newspapers at King and Bay streets, April 22, 1936.**
BACK COVER (BOTTOM): **The first Miss Toronto and runners-up at Sunnyside, 1926.**

Bill Hicks, a soldier returning from the First World War, is given a royal welcome by his family and friends, circa 1919.

For my parents,
Evelyn and Graham Cotter.

Acknowledgements

The idea for this book came from Michael Worek at Firefly Books. Further inspiration came from family and friends who lived in Toronto between the wars and were looking over my shoulder as I wrote.

I couldn't have written this book without my parents' steadfast support and constant enthusiasm. Special thanks too are due Lucinda Franco, who turns chaos into order in my house every two weeks, and my brother Sean Cotter and his wife, Nancy Warner, who gave me the idea for the phrase "the presence of the past."

At Firefly Books I would like to thank Lionel Koffler for giving me the opportunity to write the book, and my editors, Jennifer Pinfold and Dan Liebman. Bob Wilcox's design and creative juxtaposition of pictures were crucial in the development of the book, and Gillian Watts did her usual excellent job of proofreading and indexing. Thanks also to Stephen Otto for all his kind help. The staff at the Toronto City Archives were also extremely helpful and patient, and Linda Cobon at the Canadian National Exhibition Archives responded quickly and came up with some priceless information about the CNE.

Finally, thanks to my daughter, my own sweet Zoe, who is my biggest fan and loves Toronto more than anyone I know.

Contents

▲ Aunt Eleonore's house at Glengowan and Mount Pleasant Road, circa 1920s.

The Presence of the Past

When I was seven, my parents and I would visit my great-aunt Eleonore, who lived in a dark and beautiful house in Lawrence Park. I enjoyed these visits immensely, not particularly because of my aunt (a small, upright and large-bosomed woman who was distantly friendly though somewhat suspicious of children), but because of the house itself. It had a name — a romantic, full-blown name worthy of a house in a novel by L.M. Montgomery: Wyndekrest. It was a strange name for a house squeezed in beside a bridge on Mount Pleasant Road, about six feet below street level, with the front door looking directly into the wheels of the passing cars.

When the house was built in the 1920s, Mount Pleasant was much narrower and Wyndekrest stood at the crest of a small hill, with a lovely garden around it. By the 1960s only a narrow path remained between the house and the bridge. It led down to a wild ravine, where we would go to escape the grownups.

The house had its own attractions. Overshadowed by the encroaching road, it was extremely dark. The first thing you saw as you entered the sitting room was the balding head of a real brown bear who had been made into a rug and set under a grand piano. We ventured upstairs only for the bathroom, where a silver scalloped soap dish held tiny scalloped soaps. In the dark hall, closed doors hid the bedrooms.

A desk in the sitting room had bars across the side shelves, and my small hand could reach just past them to find the Niagara Falls purse made from the two crescents of a shell hinged together. A fading painting of Niagara Falls was glued to the outside of the purse; inside were red-paper compartments and, always, one silver dime.

The kitchen had a rather neglected air: long, narrow and inconvenient, and full of shadows. On each visit we had to perform the ritual of asking Aunt Eleonore politely if we could play with the things in the hoosier (an ingenious piece of kitchen furniture that combined cupboards and counter space). She would nod her head graciously, always maintaining the upright carriage that had seen her through many recitals at the Metropolitan United Church downtown, where she had been a well-known mezzo-soprano. Then we would scatter to the kitchen, settle ourselves on the floor, and lift the latch of the hoosier's lower cupboard.

Inside were all manner of exotic kitchen utensils: fluted muffin tins, cake pans, bread pans, hand mixers and many odd-shaped metal things with funny spikes and corkscrews. What were they for? We improvised, using them to cook fancy dishes, build pyramids and towers, or wage quiet wars that wouldn't attract the grownups' attention.

Aunt Eleonore's house was the first hint I had of what life in Toronto had been like in the twenties and thirties. My great-uncle, a lumber merchant, bought the newly built house in 1923, and most of the dark, dignified furniture came from Simpsons, which had the reputation of being more upscale than Eaton's. My father lived there with his aunt and uncle during school holidays in the 1930s. For me it was a ghostly house, full of memories and tantalizing glimpses of a life that was past. The piano and the bear underneath it were quiet, the kitchen utensils forgotten in a cupboard, the shadowy rooms silent and unused. I loved the idea that the house had once been something more, before the road had been widened, and that I was seeing only fragments of its true nature.

The presence of the past is all around us in Toronto, just as it was for me in the house in Lawrence Park. Within the modern city lie all the decades that came before. In houses, buildings, neighbourhoods, street names and people's memories, the Toronto of the 1920s and 1930s can still be found. Landmarks that were built then are still here: Union Station, the Eaton's College Street Building, the Bank of Commerce Building on King Street, Maple Leaf Gardens and the Royal York Hotel. Most of the street grid of the downtown core is unchanged. Many Toronto neighbourhoods were well established then, filled with houses that remain today. Many of the churches are still there, although some are now used as theatres, daycares or community centres.

Despite all the development of the downtown area in the last half of the 20th century, there are still traces of the Toronto that existed between the world wars, if you know where to look. But what about the people? Who were they? How were they different from us? How did they dress? How did they get to work? What did they do for fun?

The City of Toronto Archives, particularly the James Collection, provided me with a treasure trove of pictures of people and places from the twenties and thirties. The choices of photos and subjects in this book are personal and, in some ways, arbitrary. I did not try to cover every aspect of life in Toronto during the years between 1919 and 1939. I let the pictures lead me to the stories.

As at Wyndekrest, with its shadowed corners and truncated garden, it is possible to glimpse Toronto's past in what has survived. I hope this book will provide an opportunity to look at the present-day city and see how it is different, but still somehow the same — the vibrant city where people lived out their lives during two exciting decades when the world was poised between one devastating conflict and another.

The period between the end of the First World War and the beginning of the Second World War in Toronto is especially interesting because of the enormous changes that took place, both in the landscape of the city and in the lives of its inhabitants. These two decades were pivotal in Toronto's development from a Victorian city to the cosmopolitan metropolis it is today.

In the twenties Toronto and Canada were both finding their place in the unpredictable 20th century. Nothing stayed the same. Hemlines, music, gender roles and ways of getting around town were all transformed. The very foundation of capitalism, the stock market, displayed its unreliability in 1929 by crumbling, sending the economy into a tailspin and leaving thousands without work. Thirteen thousand Toronto men died in Europe between 1914 and 1918, and many who came back were not sure about what they had fought for. Canada had become a respected and independent nation through its contribution of men and arms to the war, and although patriotism and loyalty to Britain still ran high, Canadians' sense of themselves as Canadians (rather than as Britons living in the colonies) had grown stronger. Other values were shaken up. Women who had worked in factories while the men were away now had the vote and were not about to disappear back into the kitchen and long skirts. The young ones cut their hair, rolled down their stockings, started smoking and began going about in cars with men. Ironically, although people were loosening up their morals on every other front, the sale of liquor was prohibited until 1927. Toronto, that maiden aunt of cities, stepped cautiously into the modern world.

The twenties were in many ways the first modern decade of the 20th century, with the introduction of talking movies, the widespread use of gas and electricity and the change in attitudes to women. The pace of city life picked up after the war and never slowed down again. The automobile replaced the horse. Transportation systems amalgamated, expanded and still struggled to keep up. Airports and expressways were built. Radio, movies and mass advertising began to have a huge impact on everyday life, with the U.S. influence growing stronger.

Living conditions for the majority of Torontonians improved as slums were cleared and indoor toilets, central heating, electricity and telephones became the norm. Health care progressed, and there was a corresponding decrease in the death rate from the diseases that had ravaged the population in the previous century: tuberculosis, diphtheria, typhoid, scarlet fever

▲ A family group plus doll pose for a picture on front steps on Lincoln Avenue, June 1925.

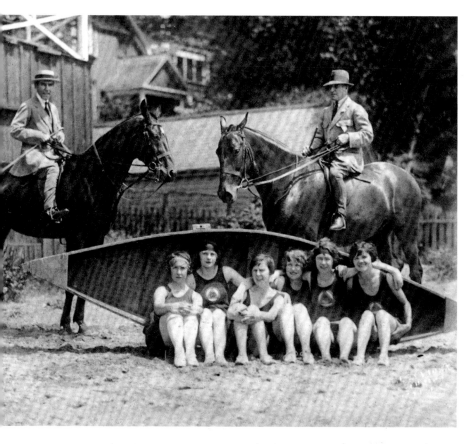

▲ **Members of the Balmy Beach Club enjoying themselves.** Their club was located at the foot of Beech Street, in the east end.

and whooping cough. Baby clinics and better child care lowered infant mortality rates.

This was a period of growth and change in Toronto, with the city expanding its services, building new housing and planning for the future. Then the Depression hit with the stock market crash of 1929, and the world tilted again. Massive unemployment rocked the foundations of society. Ordinary people saw their dreams crumble as they worked longer hours for lower wages or lost their jobs. Modern society seemed at the point of collapse. Even the royal family proved unreliable, with love (of all things) apparently triumphing over duty and the empire, when Edward VIII abdicated the throne for the questionable Wallis Simpson in 1936.

Yet Toronto, with its diversified economy and lower unemployment rate, was not as badly off as nearly everywhere else in Canada. Building projects were completed, housing standards were reformed and people survived. Life went on. Many women still put up great quantities of jam every fall, despite the availability of the commercial varieties, and men always wore hats. Eaton's had $1 sales, and people went to movies at the Uptown and watched the Dumbells at the Royal Alex. They filled their cars with gasoline and drove the new superhighway — the Queen Elizabeth Way — to Hamilton. Well-behaved Torontonians never worked on Sunday, but filled the churches instead.

Manufacturers vied for consumers with the latest models of gas stoves, wringer-washers and safety tires. Hemlines, waistlines and hair lengths went up and down. Alcohol, although prohibited for most of one decade, was always readily available. People swarmed to Sunnyside Amusement Park to swim and go on rides. They filled Maple Leaf Stadium to watch baseball. Long-distance swimming, beauty pageants and strange fads (like sitting on flagpoles for days) became popular. People went to the movies and listened to their favourite radio programs; and, in the late thirties, many Torontonians painted their houses and planted front gardens to welcome the new king and queen, as part of the "Beautify Toronto for the Royal Visit" campaign.

In the 1920s and 1930s Canada's identity was still intimately tied to Britain. The three royal visits during this time were met with wild enthusiasm. The presence of the royal figures not only reinforced patriotic feeling toward England, but also provided everyone in the city with excitement and entertainment.

In 1921, 85 percent of Torontonians were of British ancestry. The remaining 15 percent was split among Jews (the largest group, at about 6 percent), Italians, French, Finns, Greeks, Macedonians, Chinese, Japanese and blacks. Prejudice and racism were accepted by the majority of Canadians. Jews were banned from beaches and hotels, and the middle class did their best to keep them out of their professions. There were very few Jewish teachers, university professors, nurses, doctors or architects. White, Anglo-Saxon Protestants formed the majority in Toronto between the wars. British values and patriotism were encouraged throughout society and particularly at schools, with "God Save the King" as the national anthem and textbooks filled with British references. Children of immigrants were moulded as quickly and firmly as possible into little British-loving Canadians, no matter what their provenance.

Eighty-five percent of Torontonians were Protestants, with Anglicans claiming the most souls and the Presbyterians and the Methodists ranking second and third. Although some Presbyterians dissented, in 1925 these latter two Protestant groups joined forces with the Congregationalists to become the United Church of Canada. There were two services every Sunday at Toronto churches and, with the blue laws in full force, everything but church shut down tight all day. Even tobogganing in High Park on Sunday was strictly forbidden. Ernest Hemingway famously complained that he couldn't buy a box of chocolates for a sick friend at a drugstore on a Sunday in Toronto in the mid-1920s.

The *Ontario Temperance Act* came into effect in 1916 and lasted until 1927, when the *Liquor Control Act* was passed. During Prohibition, as this period was called, all bars, liquor stores and clubs were closed down. People were allowed to keep liquor in their own homes, as long as they had bought it outside the province. Otherwise, would-be drinkers went to bootleggers or to one of the scores of willing doctors who wrote prescriptions for medicinal alcohol use. Toronto was dry, but not parched.

Looking back from the perspective of today, these two decades take on a certain poignancy, framed as they were between the shadows of the two world wars. Torontonians struggled to live and work in the midst of social upheaval, changing moral codes, the Depression and the growing pains of the expanding city. The pictures that follow and the stories that accompany them provide a window into that time and place.

Life in the City
1919-1939

◄ **Selling newspapers at King and Bay streets, April 22, 1936.** This picture is interesting not only for the downtown bustle it has captured, but also for the inaccuracy of the dramatic message on the newspaper. The men trapped in the Moose River mine were not to be brought to the surface until midday on April 23, and the afternoon papers of the day before jumped the gun by about 24 hours. The following day, after the men had been finally released from their ordeal, the *Globe* issued an extra edition with the smug headline, "Really Rescued,"

Toronto had been in the grip of the Moose River mine drama for 11 days. Inch-by-inch radio coverage kept the public suspended with hope and dread, much the way people follow disasters today on television. It all began on April 12, when three Toronto businessmen, Dr. D.E. Robertson, Alfred Scadding and Herman Magill, descended into the abandoned Moose River gold mine in Nova Scotia to determine whether it could be resuscitated. A sudden rockslide trapped them 141 feet below the surface. News of the emergency spread quickly across the country and, while three hundred draegermen (coal miners specially trained for rescue work) worked day and night to reach the victims, their painstaking progress was broadcast nationally by J. Frank Willis, an announcer with a rich voice and a dramatic delivery.

Six days after the rockslide, the rescue workers managed to drill a hole down to the trapped men, and they could hear faint voices. Two days later the news was shouted up the pipe that Magill had died and their prison was filling with water. It was a tricky rescue. If they moved too fast, the draegermen could cause another rock slide; too cautiously, and the entrapped men would be dead by the time they were reached. Finally, on April 26, 10 days after the men had been trapped, rescue seemed imminent and the Toronto papers jumped the gun. The next day the survivors were

brought up into the daylight just before 1 p.m. The rescue crew, led by the Salvation Army, removed their hats and sang the doxology ("Praise God from Whom All Blessings Flow"). In Toronto, the bells at City Hall pealed out and people ran joyfully into the streets, laughing and crying. The city had been released from one of the first media-enhanced dramas of the century.

PREVIOUS PAGE: **This crowd has gathered to watch the first Miss Toronto beauty contest, Sunnyside Amusement Park, August 1926.**

▲ **Red Lake prospectors, March 1926.** These three gents have a good reason to smile. In 1925 they registered mining claims in Red Lake, northwestern Ontario, and became very, very rich. Their discovery of gold inspired more than one thousand prospectors to head north. In the twenties and thirties mining in northern Ontario fuelled the Toronto economy, and by the 1940s there were 12 producing mines in the Red Lake area. In 1926, a skyscraper called the Northern Ontario Building was completed at Bay and Adelaide to house the offices of mining companies.

A policeman directs traffic at Yonge and Bloor streets, December 11, 1923. He functions as a human traffic light, with his "Stop" and "Go" signs mounted on a pole. Automatic lights were introduced to Toronto streets in 1925, with the first one installed at this intersection. The building in the background (the southwest corner) was the original Stollery's menswear shop, rebuilt in 1929 after the street was widened.

► **Looking south from Queen and Yonge.** In the 19th century King Street was the main commercial artery of the city, with all the best shops and businesses located there. By 1900 the growth of substantial businesses along Yonge Street made it a close second, and the intersection of King and Yonge was the heart of downtown. But in the twenties and thirties the centre shifted to Queen and Yonge, with theatres and the large Eaton's and Simpsons department stores dominating that intersection.

◀ **Grecian dance was another fad of the twenties, with costumes and postures borrowed from classical forms.** It was influenced strongly by Isadora Duncan, the grandmother of modern dance, who at the turn of the century had introduced the world to a new form of interpretative dance that deviated from the traditional forms of ballet. Isadora and her followers danced barefoot, wearing loose-fitting tunics reminiscent of classical Greek costume.

▶ **This young lady's daring attire is for a masquerade at the Ski Club, April 1926.** Masquerades were highly popular parties in the twenties, with people going to great expense and trouble to buy or make their costumes.

▲ **Even during the Depression, wealthy people had to find some amusement.** An elegant roadster and a photogenic wolfhound were fashion accessories that only the very rich could afford. This woman — a fur around her neck and a furry friend at her side — keeps warm in her open car outside the Eglinton Hunt Club. The club stood at the corner of Avenue Road and Roselawn Avenue, just north of Eglinton Avenue.

► **The Toronto Stock Exchange, Bay Street south of King, late 1930s.** In 1937 the exquisite, evocative Art Deco Toronto Stock Exchange Building rose much like a phoenix from the ashes of the Depression. By 1935 it seemed as if the worst of the Depression was over and, in a gesture of hope, the exchange decided to build a new facility incorporating the rapidly changing technology of its trade and the bold design features of Art Deco and Art Moderne. The result was this gem, built with smoky pink granite and pale Indiana limestone and marked by five stunning tall windows and a 74-foot-wide decorative stone frieze by Charles Comfort, which historians Dendy and Kilbourn have described as "the most striking piece of sculpture from the period in Toronto."

Founded in 1852 and incorporated in 1878, the Toronto Stock Exchange moved to new premises built on this site in 1911. During the investment boom of the twenties, the facilities became overcrowded and, by 1936, the new exchange was in the planning stage. George and Moorhouse, the architects, with S.H. Maw as associate architect, designed a building that was thoroughly modern in form and function. During the twenties and thirties the volume of shares traded increased dramatically, aided by updated communication methods that included telephone, telegraph, tickertape and pneumatic tubes. The new exchange building was created with all this in mind.

The tall windows that dominate the façade overlook the three-storey trading floor inside, which is 39 feet tall and 72 by 105 feet wide, with galleries at each end of the room. The walls are decorated in Art Deco style with pale marble, opal glass, silver and wood. Charles Comfort painted eight Cubist-style murals, each 16 feet high, depicting the major industries of Canada.

Comfort's frieze above the doors on the outside of the building is worked in gold-coloured stone, with stylized figures of workers and their machines toiling in the industries traded at the exchange.

◀ **Eaton's College Street, southwest corner of College and Yonge streets, circa 1930.** This building was originally planned as one of the most ambitious construction projects ever attempted in Toronto. The architects were Ross & Macdonald (with Sproatt and Rolph) — the same firms that were involved in the designs for the Royal York Hotel. The plan was to build a 36-storey skyscraper to house an elegant new Eaton's store and bring the company's offices and factories under one roof. But the Depression hit Toronto in the second year of construction, and what was to have been the base of the skyscraper became Eaton's College Street store. Although it did not dominate the Toronto skyline the way the architects had hoped it would, the seven-storey store provided a good example of a classic Art Deco commercial building, constructed of limestone and granite, with bronze details.

Sir John Craig Eaton (also known as Jack) believed that College and Yonge would become the heart of a fashionable uptown district, picking up crosstown business from its position at the intersection of Yonge, Carlton and College streets. He planned his store to be the first major development project there. As part of his strategy, the plans were kept so secret that, although Eaton's had been buying up land around College and Yonge for 20 years, local realtors believed that the property had been acquired by Marshall Field's of Chicago. Eaton's donated some of the land to the city to have the street widened and the Carlton/College jog smoothed. Unfortunately, despite the relative success of the College Street store and the lure of the glamorous seventh floor, the area never did become a mecca for the carriage trade. Sir John had miscalculated by about half a mile. Yonge and Bloor would have been perfect.

▲ **The pedestrian arcade on the first floor of the Eaton's College Street store, 1930.** René Cera, one of Eaton's staff architects, designed the first floor to accommodate the change in grade along Yonge Street. Elegant staircases led from the pedestrian arcade on the lower level to a spacious retail space on the upper one. The marble, travertine and other rich materials on one level matched those on the other, as did the lighting. The streamlined Art Deco style is apparent in the design details and in the use of rich materials such as marble, travertine and nickel alloys.

▼ **The "Foodateria" in the basement of Eaton's Queen Street store, circa 1936.** Buying your groceries at Eaton's was part of the one-stop-shopping department store concept. These two employees were lucky to have jobs during the Depression. Eaton's, along with the rest of the country, suffered its share of Depression casualties. The store's sales dropped drastically, especially during 1931 and 1932, when annual losses exceeded $2 million. The company tried to deal with the losses by cutting wages and hours. Married women were expected to give up their jobs to men who were supporting families.

▶ **The Round Room restaurant on the seventh floor of Eaton's College Street, 1930.** Lady Eaton happily declared the Eaton's College Street store open in October 1930, one year after the fatal stock market crash of 1929. The Depression had begun, but many people thought it would not last. Nobody knew the depths to which the economy would sink — or the hardships that Canadians would endure — in the coming years.

The luxurious seventh floor opened in March 1931, geared unabashedly toward the rich. Jacques Carlu's designs for the Round Room touched on every detail, including wall coverings, furniture, linen, china, silverware — and even the uniforms of the serving staff. The colours were cool and sophisticated: beige, taupe and pale yellow with silver and black accents. The fountain in the centre of the room was a masterpiece of black granite and black vitrolite glass. Indirect lighting enhanced the sophisticated ambiance. An interesting feature added a frisson of eavesdropping excitement to an expensive lunch. Rumour had it that, thanks to the acoustics of the circular room, diners could hear the intimate conversations of customers on the other side of the restaurant. Five years after Carlu designed the Round Room, he created the famous Rainbow Room on the 65th floor of Manhattan's Rockefeller Plaza.

◀ **The Royal York Hotel, from the southeast, circa 1929.** A landmark since its opening in 1929, the Royal York was built on the site of another impressive building, the Queen's Hotel, which graced Front Street between 1844 and 1927. The Queen's had been a social centre for Torontonians, and had housed most of the city's famous guests.

The new hotel set out to be the best and the biggest, and in many respects it succeeded. One of the CPR's series of railway hotels (which included, among others, the Château Frontenac in Quebec, the Banff Springs and Château Lake Louise in Alberta, and the Empress in Victoria), it was planned as a counterpoint to Union Station, with a tunnel under Front Street that connected the two buildings. When it was completed the Royal York held the record as the largest hotel in the British Commonwealth, with 1,600 rooms (all with running water), and came with a final price tag of $18 million. The biggest central heating plant in Canada provided heat for the hotel, Union Station and all the buildings on the south side of Front Street between Yonge and Simcoe streets.

▶ **The Canadian Bank of Commerce Building on King Street, looking southeast, circa 1931.** This classic skyscraper is a splendid example of the Beaux Arts architectural movement of the late 19th and early 20th centuries that left its mark on Front Street in the form of Union Station and the Dominion Public Building. Like a medieval cathedral with its arched entrance at street level and a decorated tower reaching into the sky, the Commerce Building invites worshippers to enter and offer their devotions, although here the reverence is to the God of money and industry, not Christianity.

The completion of the building in 1931 changed the Toronto skyline forever. By day with its great height and by night with the illumination of its crest, the 476-foot-high tower stood as a beacon of stately progress and proclaimed the city's aspirations to greatness, or at least to tall buildings. The architects, York and Sawyer, were well known for their bank buildings in New York City, which by this time was a forest of sky-scrapers. In Toronto, they helped to create what was billed as "the tallest building in the British Empire."

Ascending from a seven-storey base, the office tower of 34 storeys rises in a series of setbacks to the observation terrace. There, looking out over the city, are four giant heads — representing courage, observation, foresight and enterprise. With its unique vantage point high above all the other downtown buildings, the terrace proved a favourite destination for tourists and Torontonians alike.

The entrance on King Street champions additional capitalist virtues. Two female figures on a panel above the main doors personify industry and commerce, accompanied by Mercury, the god of bankers. In the background are depictions of a grain elevator, the outline of the Commerce Building, and five Canada geese suspended in flight. The entrance arch is decorated with various animals that symbolize thrift and industry: bears, squirrels, roosters and bees.

The main banking hall was modelled on the Baths of Caracalla in Rome. It features a deep-blue coffered vault ceiling that measures 65 feet at its apex, walls made of roseate stone, and gilt mouldings. The room is 145 feet long and 85 feet wide.

▼ Looking east from Front and York streets along the façade of Union Station, circa 1935. Regal, majestic, a temple to the transcontinental railway and the industry that built it — Union Station can be described by a list of superlatives. But to Torontonians in the 1920s, the building was the object of a running joke. Virtually completed in 1920 but not fully functional until 1930, it stood as a monument to petty squabbling and political manoeuvring between the city government and the two railway lines that gave rise to the name "Union." The problem was that the players could not agree on a very basic principle: should the tracks coming into the station be raised or at ground level? Level crossings at Bay and York would cause endless traffic holdups, but who was gonna pay for the bridges? There were many other causes for delay, but the cost of raising the tracks lay at the heart of the debate.

In 1905, when the planning got underway for Union Station, trains and railways were in their heyday. The automobile had yet to threaten their dominion over transportation across North America. Railway stations assumed monumental proportions.

In New York City, Pennsylvania Station opened in 1911, with Grand Central following two years later. Union Station was planned as a similar temple to modern transportation, but the project was plagued with innumerable delays, including the lack of materials, finances and labour during the First World War and the endless squabbling between the principals during the teens and twenties. The station was conceived when the Canadian Pacific Railway (CPR) and the Grand Trunk Railway were the major players, but by 1923 the Grand Trunk was no more and Canadian National Railways had stepped into the debate.

Meanwhile, the station that was supposed to take three years to build was finally completed in 25. Although the Prince of Wales opened the station officially in 1927 (extremely quickly, in a ceremony that lasted less than 15 minutes), it was only in 1930 that all the trains actually stopped there. To board their trains, passengers had to struggle with their bags from the ticket office at the new Union Station through various corridors to the old Union Station tracks (on Station Street, west of York Street and south of Front). An enterprising reporter once measured the longest distance between ticket booths and trains at one-quarter of a mile.

But despite its considerable growing pains, Union Station remains one of the architectural gems bequeathed to Toronto from the twenties. The gracious Beaux Arts temple still defines the streetscape. Most of the credit for the design goes to John M. Lyle. Front Street had to be widened by 25 feet to accommodate the scope of the façade, and then the building was set back another 47 feet from the curb. Each of the 22 pillars along the baroque Roman façade is 40 feet tall and weighs 75 tons.

The Great Hall was modelled partly after the Santa Maria Maggiore church in Rome (432 A.D.), with the coffered, tiled ceiling echoing the original. The other major influence was the hall of the imperial baths of Rome. Four-storey-high arched windows at each end, along with rows of clerestory windows, let in natural light to illuminate the fine grey and pink marble floors and the sand-coloured stone walls. At 260 feet long and 90 feet high, the Great Hall was the largest room in Toronto at the time. Along the frieze, just below the ceiling, run the names of Canadian cities connected by trains from this station, a homage to the power and grandeur of the transcontinental railway.

◄ **Steam engines at the eastern entrance to Union Station, with the Royal York Hotel in the background, circa 1929.** By the time the Royal York Hotel was completed in 1929, Union Station had opened officially, after years of wrangling between the railway companies and the city. Some final rail connections were still to be made, but from this photograph it's clear that the station was operational. With the dynamic engines belching steam in the foreground and the imposing hotel rising majestically in the background, the scene conveys the fact that Toronto has at last taken its place as a vital North American city. It is ironic that this image of progress and stability was recorded on the brink of the Depression. The economy that formed the base of Toronto's success was about to plunge into uncertainty.

◀ **Vehicles wait at a level crossing, possibly on Dundas Street West, circa 1927.** This picture illustrates photographer William James's ability to capture a moment of action on film. As the cars (and horse) wait in stillness, the train thunders past, belching black steam. A second later the engine will be gone, but for the moment it is frozen in time. There is something about the juxtaposition of the horse, the cars, the dynamic engine and the glimpse of the coal company's sign that conveys the spirit of the times: progress is rumbling forward, with the past represented by the lone and patient horse.

▲ **British American Oil Company garage on the northwest corner of Front and Sherbourne streets, 1930s.** By the time this gas station was built, someone had realized the advantages of operating a gas station that included space off the road where cars could fill up, a couple of pumps to serve more than one vehicle at a time, and a garage for repairs. The two trucks using the station are service vehicles, one for a laundry and the other for a plumbing business. In 1929 the City of Toronto stopped issuing licences for sidewalk gas pumps, and this kind of station became the norm. With the tremendous growth in car ownership that followed the war, gas was in short supply. The price rose dramatically, from 17 cents a gallon (about 4 cents a litre) in 1915 to 45.5 cents (about 10 cents) in 1920. But by 1927, despite a provincial gas tax imposed in 1925, the price had dropped to 27.8 cents a gallon (about 6 cents a litre).

◀ **Improvements being made to an unidentified intersection transected by the Yonge streetcar.** When the Toronto Transportation Commission took over the recalcitrant Toronto Railway Company in 1920, it faced the enormous challenge of updating an old and inefficient system. The new commission prided itself on working quickly with as little disruption as possible to traffic and pedestrians. Often the TTC would rebuild an entire intersection between the end of the late-afternoon rush hour and the start of the one the next morning. The intersection at Yonge and Queen was transformed overnight, with old tracks and pavement ripped up and new tracks installed. Perhaps the most complicated intersection in the city was the "union" of the three sets of tracks that met at Queen Street, King Street and Roncesvalles Avenue. The TTC built the intersection in a construction yard, dismantled it and then rebuilt it onsite in nine hours.

IN SERVICE BEFORE 1891

▶ **An original Toronto Railway Company horsecar is pulled up Black Creek Hill on Weston Road, November 28, 1925.** The spectacle is part of a parade to celebrate TTC service coming to Weston with the expansion of modern-day streetcar service along Weston Road. In 1925 a horse-drawn streetcar was a novelty to the eager little boys who followed it up this hill, but 35 years earlier it was a common sight. From 1861 until 1894, Toronto commuters were carried by horsecars like this one run by the Toronto Street Railway Company (TSRC). Toronto's city council must have had a weakness for 30-year agreements for its transit systems; it signed one in 1861 with the TSRC and, almost as soon as it was released in 1891, it signed up with the Toronto

Railway Company for another 30 years.

When the TSRC began its monopoly in 1861, eleven cars ran on three streetcar lines in the city: along Yonge Street from King to Bloor; along Queen Street from Yonge to the Lunatic Asylum (at Ossington); and along King Street from the Don River to Bathurst. The fare was five cents a ride, with no transfers, and the service ran 16 hours in the winter and 14 in the summer, six days a week. There was no Sunday service because of the strict blue laws that restricted business and many other activities. The horse-drawn cars were not allowed to move faster than six miles per hour (compared with the 25 miles per hour that today's streetcars average), and the heating system consisted of straw heaped on the floor to

keep the customers' feet warm. When the snow was really deep, cars were replaced with sleighs. By the end of its franchise, the TSRC was running 262 cars, pulled by a total of 1,372 horses along 68 miles of track. The horses left their calling cards everywhere, filling Toronto's air with the pungent smell of "road apples."

When the Toronto Railway Company negotiated its franchise in 1891, quick electrification was one of the major conditions of the agreement. The first electric streetcar appeared on Toronto streets in 1892, and the last horses were laid off in 1894. The new streetcars used rather inefficient coal stoves for heat and had replaceable bodies: closed in winter, and open "toast-rack" style in summer.

▼ **Houses under construction in Forest Hill, January 1936.** Forest Hill came into its own in the age of the automobile. Many middle-class professionals with money had previously been content to live in large houses in the Annex. But in the 1920s they started moving north to enjoy the more rarefied air beyond the Davenport hill. With new roads being built and old roads being paved, it became quite reasonable to commute to work and return at night to the peaceful enclave, far from the bustle of downtown. The Annex grew somewhat shabbier, with many homes divided into apartments and boarding houses as the Depression took its toll on homeowners.

Forest Hill, incorporated in 1924, established its prestige as a respectable and moneyed neighbourhood by legislating housing standards from the outset. Subject to size restrictions and setback regulations, each new home had a tree planted in the front. In 1931 the residents voted in a referendum for an increase in taxes that would keep industry out of the area, and a 1936 bylaw decreed that any new residences had to be designed by an architect and meet the approval of a team of professionals. In 1953 Forest Hill became part of the Municipality of Metropolitan Toronto. However, until it was amalgamated into the City of Toronto in 1967, it continued to maintain a degree of independence.

▶ **This car is stuck in the mud on the still-unpaved Brentwood Road, near Kingsway Park, March 1936.** Like Forest Hill, Kingsway Park was developed in the 1920s and 1930s as a model suburb with strict architectural guidelines. Robert Home Smith was the developer who transformed 3,000 acres north of the mouth of the Humber River into a gracious neighbourhood of winding streets, carefully landscaped lots, and olde-English–style houses, many using Tudor half-timbering.

Reconstructed streetcars on the Bathurst Street route, July 18, 1923.

◀ **Looking north on Bay Street to City Hall, 1920s.** Bay Street underwent a transformation in the 1920s and early 1930s with the construction of a series of skyscrapers. The Northern Ontario Building went up in 1926 at Adelaide and Bay streets. The marvellous Art Deco Canada Permanent Trust Building, also at Adelaide and Bay, was completed in 1929. At Bay and Richmond was the Sterling Tower (1928). Just off Bay were the Victory Building (1930) on Richmond, the Toronto Star Building (1929) on King, and the Concourse Building (1928) on Adelaide.

The queen of skyscrapers, the Canadian Bank of Commerce Building, was built on King just east of Bay in 1931.

▼ **Traffic jam on York Street north of Adelaide, 1931.** By the end of the twenties the automobile had taken over the streets of Toronto. Although horses were used into the thirties and even the forties, for the most part the car was king. The transformation of Toronto from a sleepy Victorian city to a modern industrial centre took about 30 years, and the car was the galvanizing force

behind the change. It required paved roads, gas stations, bridges, traffic lights and signs, speed limits, licences and various regulations. Toronto's capital expenses grew from $5.6 million at the turn of the century to $82.5 million in 1930, and the changes in the city to accommodate cars made up a large part of the extra expense. But Torontonians revelled in the age of the automobile, and their enthusiasm could not be dampened by traffic jams, horrendous accidents or steep gas taxes.

► **Aerial view of downtown Toronto, circa 1930.** The 1920s could be dubbed the decade in which Toronto discovered the skyscraper. Although several had been built earlier, skyscrapers proliferated in the twenties. Seven went up downtown between 1922 and 1927, and seven more in 1928 alone.

In this aerial view of Toronto, the Royal York Hotel and the Canadian Bank of Commerce Building dominate the skyline, as they would do for another 40 years. They can still be glimpsed together in all their golden splendour from certain points on the Gardiner expressway — sentinels from another time, crowded and almost blocked from view by the super-skyscrapers of the last third of the 20th century.

In 1919 only a few buildings in Toronto could legitimately be called "skyscrapers." Built in a classic, columnar style, with a weighty base and a series of floors that rose vertically to a decorated cornice, these buildings were mostly found on Yonge Street. A zoning bylaw in New York City in 1916 had resulted in the creation of the stepped profile, as best represented by the Empire State Building. The bylaw was concerned with restricting bulk according to height, making it necessary for buildings to become narrower as they grew taller. A series of skyscrapers rising one after another on Bay Street in the twenties drew comparisons with the New York "canyons," where light and sky were blocked. The Bay Street Canyon, along with City Hall, Eaton's and Simpsons, became a point of reference for the heart of downtown.

As is evident in this picture, west of Bay Street and east of Yonge the skyline dropped off dramatically in height.

1. Old City Hall
2. St. Michael's Cathedral
3. Metropolitan United Church
4. St. James's Cathedral
5. Canadian Bank of
   Commerce Building
6. Royal York Hotel
7. Union Station
8. Front Street
9. Wellington Street
10. King Street
11. Adelaide Street
12. Richmond Street
13. Queen Street

▼ This photo was labelled as the first newsreel truck to appear in Toronto, probably at the Thorncliffe racetrack, circa 1929. Sound came to the movies in 1927, when William Fox released the first comedy with spoken dialogue. The same year saw him produce the first newsreels with sound. Newsreels were standard fare in movie theatres throughout the twenties and thirties, showing highlights of the most recent news.

▶ Newspapermen at work in the *Toronto Star* newsroom at 80 King Street West, 1930. This building was another skyscraper that appeared in the late twenties. The 23-storey Toronto Star Building was completed in 1929. From its labour-influenced beginnings, the *Toronto Star* maintained its reputation as the most liberal of Toronto's newspapers. It supported William Lyon Mackenzie King and his federal Liberals and was firmly behind the principles of free speech, limited social welfare and free trade. The *Star* stood in direct opposition to its most bitter rival, the anti-red, occasionally racist *Telegram*, which championed taxation restraint, the Conservatives and protectionism. The two dailies were deeply and often acrimoniously involved in city politics, along with the other major Toronto newspapers, the *Globe* and the *Mail and Empire*.

49

◀ **Boys gathering outside a movie theatre on Dundas Street, September 1923.** Throughout the twenties and thirties, movies provided cheap entertainment for young and old alike. Many new movie houses were built in the 1930s, among them the big ones like the Hollywood and the Uptown, as well as smaller neighbourhood theatres like the one pictured here. The talkies were officially introduced in 1927, and some of the memorable hits of the era were Charlie Chaplin's *City Lights* and *Modern Times,* Greta Garbo's *Grand Hotel* and *Camille,* and *King Kong* with Canada's own Fay Wray.

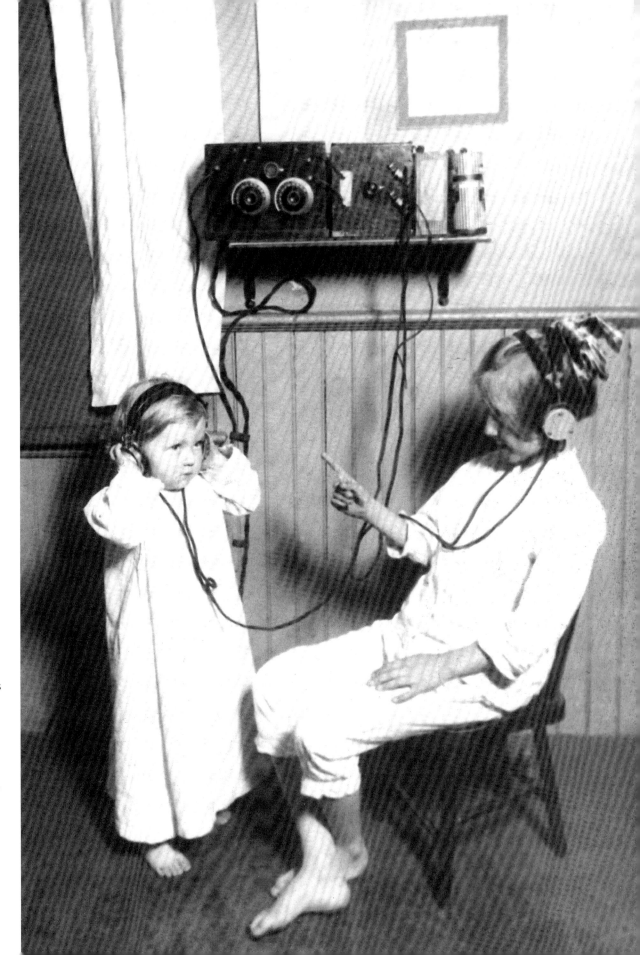

◄ **The *Toronto Star* radio truck at the Canadian National Exhibition, 1922.** The interesting thing about this picture is what you *can't* see: the sounds emanating from the loudspeaker that everyone is listening to. Radio came to Toronto in the early twenties, bringing music, news, sports, advertising and even church services right into people's homes. Suddenly Torontonians were connected with the wider world. This truck was the pride of CFCA, the *Toronto Star* radio station. The photo was taken at the first public demonstration in Toronto of the wonders of radio. The truck was fitted with special equipment that allowed it to receive radio broadcasts and transmit them from the loudspeaker on the roof. The idea was to advertise the marvels of radio broadcasting, and the truck drew bystanders like a magnet.

▶ **These two little girls are listening through headphones to an early radio broadcast, circa 1924.** Not all radios had speakers. In the early days of radio, most stations were on the air for only a few hours a day, or sometimes just on weekends. About 10 private radio stations operated in the Toronto area. They were owned by different businesses, including Eaton's, newspapers and a bond brokerage firm. Live hockey broadcasts from Maple Leaf Gardens with Foster Hewitt began in 1932, and the popular CFRB daily news was broadcast at 8 a.m. and 6 p.m. In the thirties, favourite CBC radio shows included two dance music programs (*Billy Bissett's Orchestra from the Royal York* and *The Old Mill Orchestra*) and *Forgotten Footsteps,* an archaelogy series, based on artifacts from the Royal Ontario Museum. All programs were broadcast live.

▼ **Adding-machine staff calculate election results on the night of the federal election, September 14, 1926.** This was the second federal election in 11 months, caused by a constitutional crisis involving the governor general, Lord Byng. After the October 1925 election, William Lyon Mackenzie King and his Liberal party formed a minority government with the support of the Progressives. This support proved unreliable and, in June 1926, King asked Byng to dissolve the government and call an election. An English aristocrat somewhat insensitive to Canadian nationalistic feeling, Byng chose to reject King's request and asked the opposition leader, Arthur Meighen, to form a government with his Conservatives. The new government lasted only three days, and Byng was forced to call an election. King recorded his glee in his diary. He could not believe that Lord Byng "would deliver himself so completely into my hands ... Spent the last hour tonight singing hymns." Although Byng's actions were not technically wrong, they had the appearance of interference from Britain — and virtually guaranteed King the next election. King appealed to Canadians' sense of themselves as an independent nation and was returned to power with a majority.

▶ **Reporters at City Hall on the night of the federal election, September 14, 1926.**

Officers from the traffic division line up with their motorcycles on the south side of Dundas Street West, 1928. The Toronto Police Department purchased its first four motorcycles in 1913. By 1928 the traffic division had 19. Here Police Chief Draper stands proudly with his officers east of Police Station #2 on Dundas, just west of University Avenue.

◄ **South African War memorial at Queen Street and University Avenue, circa 1921.** Walter S. Allward, who would later design the impressive World War I monument at Vimy, France, created this memorial in 1911 to commemorate the Canadian soldiers who lost their lives during the Boer War in South Africa (1899–1902). It was placed a stone's throw from the Armouries on University Avenue, which served as a rallying point for soldiers for both the world wars of the 20th century. The memorial served as a sober reminder of war throughout the twenties and thirties.

► **A veteran in the Naval Parade, March 1936.**

◄ **Veterans march in the Warriors' Day Parade at the Canadian National Exhibition, August 28, 1926.** The war of 1914–18 was very much present in Toronto during the twenties and thirties. Reminders included the annual veterans' parades and the memorial built in front of City Hall. Less tangible were the changes that the conflict had wrought. The roughly 500,000 Canadian soldiers who fought in Europe left behind a world where values were straightforward and everyone knew their place. The veterans who returned found a society transformed. In most provinces, women had the vote. Cities were rapidly expanding, the government had imposed a federal income tax, the railway had been nationalized and the country was deeply in debt. Canada's involvement in the war had gained the country a place in international affairs. Given high inflation, a shortage of work and the shining example of the Russian Revolution, social unrest was stirring. Nothing was simple any more.

▼ **Upper Canada College cadet review, May 1925.**

▲ **Edward, Prince of Wales, greets dignitaries during his visit to Toronto, August 1919.** Just nine months after the war ended, the Prince of Wales made a state visit to Canada. The visit not only celebrated the victory of Britain and its allies against the Germans, but also reinforced the ties between Canada and Britain at a time when Canadians' faith in the British Empire had been shaken by the horrors of the war. Edward was very popular in Canada. For much of the visit, the prince wore khaki, a reminder of the war and his active role in it. Edward made a number of public appearances and was met everywhere with enthusiastic crowds. He opened the Canadian National Exhibition and the Prince Edward Viaduct (quickly renamed in his honour), visited wounded veterans, went to hospitals and attended a dance at the Royal Canadian Yacht Club, where he caused many a maiden's heart to flutter by his choice of dance partners. One of the more unusual events he attended was the beginning of the Great Toronto–New York Air Race at the Leaside Aerodrome, sponsored by the CNE. Most of the aircraft, including some bombers and training planes, were remnants of the war. The race was marked with mishap, with many of the airplanes crashing and breaking up. Fortunately, and miraculously, there were no fatalities.

On August 27, to say goodbye to the people of Toronto, the prince drove along a 20-mile route through the city, with 50,000 spectators cheering him on. Edward returned to Canada in 1927, accompanied by his brother Albert (later George VI), inspiring similar excitement. His abdication in December 1936 came as a great blow to the people who had given him much of their hope and affection.

▲ **David Lloyd George (far right), former prime minister of Great Britain, on the podium at City Hall during a visit to Toronto, October 1923.** With Lloyd George's election as British prime minister in 1916, a significant change took place in Canada's war role. Previously, Canadian soldiers were welcome, but Canadian participation in the decisions and direction of the troops was not. Lloyd George recognized the enormous contribution of the "Dominions" (Canada, Australia, New Zealand and South Africa) and invited the Canadian prime minister, Robert Borden, to the next war conference. As a result of Canada's active participation in the war, the country emerged from the conflict as a nation in its own right.

◄ **A crowd on the University of Toronto campus waits to catch a glimpse of Edward, Prince of Wales, 1927.** The Stewart Observatory and University College are in the background. This was Edward's second official visit to Toronto (the first was in 1919, just after the war). He arrived with his brother, Prince Albert, the Duke of York (who would become King George VI in 1936, with Edward's abdication of the throne). The princes presided at the opening of the Princes' Gates at the Canadian National Exhibition, which were named in their honour. The highly popular Edward was greeted by enthusiastic crowds everywhere he went.

▼ **Flappers walk down a busy Toronto street.** The bobbed hair, cloche hats and short dresses with dropped waists were trademarks of twenties' style. The underwear required to achieve the flat, boyish figure that the look depended on was quite intriguing. Eaton's catalogue of 1927 offered "Brassieres, Bandeaus and Corselettes" as well as traditional corsets and girdles, all designed to mould and flatten various female figures into perpendicular lines. The corselette was particularly suited to the current fashion, with elastic and boning from bust to hips for that streamlined effect.

▶ Looking east along Queen Street, just west of Yonge, 1920s. Simpsons is on the right and Eaton's and Woolworth's on the left.

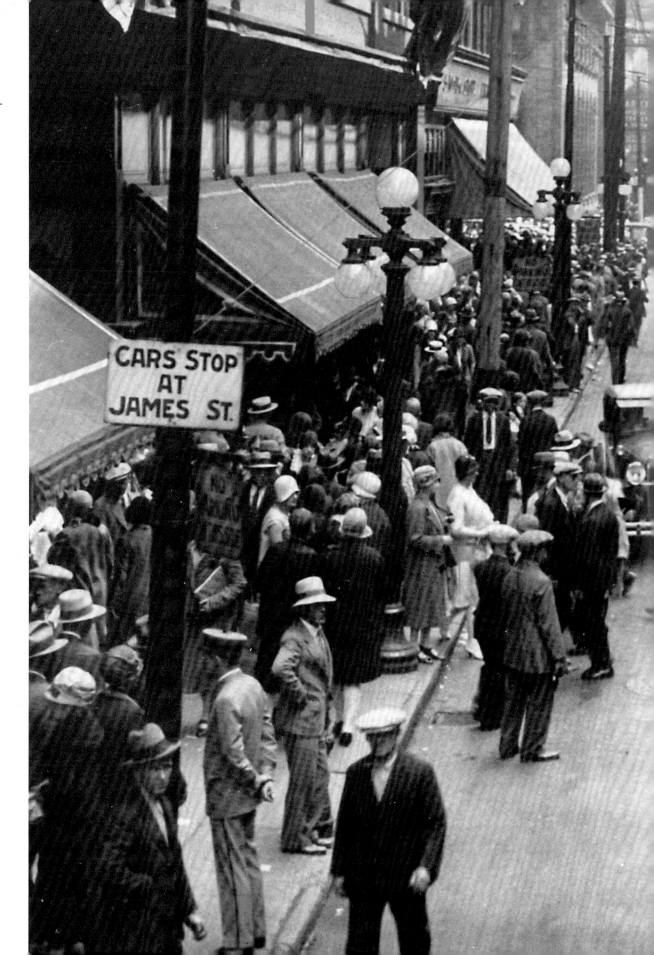

► **A row of rather seedy enterprises — pawnshops, cigar stores, printers, a café and the Vaudeville Theatre — line the south side of Queen Street, circa 1925.** This picture looks east to Bay Street, where the domes of the Temple Building are just visible. This part of Queen Street marked the lower border of the infamous Ward, home to various immigrant groups over the years. At about this time, the Ward was changing from being largely Jewish to Chinese and Italian, as many Jews either moved west of University Avenue into the streets near Kensington Market or bought property elsewhere in the city. Two Chinese newspapers had their offices near here in the thirties: the *Shing Wah Daily News* on Queen Street, and the *Chinese Times* on Elizabeth Street.

▲ **In 1927, University Avenue ended here at Queen Street.** It was not extended to Front Street until 1931. Although the classically inspired Osgoode Hall was on the northeast corner, with the Armouries just beyond, and City Hall reigned over Queen and Bay a couple of blocks east, this part of Queen Street remained fairly seedy. It formed the southern border of the Ward, known for its poor housing conditions and overcrowding.

▶ During the streetcar strike in 1919, people travelled by any possible means. Anyone with an available truck or car, it seemed, transformed the vehicle into a jitney and made a fortune transporting stranded commuters.

▼ Men crowd into the back of a truck during the streetcar strike in 1919.

◄ **Desperate to get to work, these commuters crowd around a jitney, hoping to squeeze in, during the streetcar strike in the summer of 1919.** In 1919 the country seethed with labour unrest. The economy was struggling in the aftermath of the war, and soldiers who had returned from the horror of the trenches had trouble finding work. Inflation was high, and men who had seen their friends fall and had sacrificed their youth (and often their health) on European soil were disillusioned with the society they had fought to maintain.

The Russian Revolution of 1917 inspired labour unrest and gave rise to great uneasiness among politicians and the Canadian business class. Trade unions, which had grown significantly in number and membership, demanded that employers negotiate with them. On May 13, 1919, the Winnipeg General Strike was called by the Trades and Labour Council when the employers of metal workers refused to bargain collectively for better wages. The city came to a halt as 35,000 workers went on strike. Passive resistance gave way to street marches. The government cracked down on June 17, arresting eight of the leaders. When on June 21 a crowd gathered outside Winnipeg's city hall to protest this action, mounted police rode through the protesters, shooting. The police killed two and wounded many more, and the general strike was over.

The rest of the country monitored the drama in Winnipeg. Some were afraid that Bolshevism would take hold and overthrow the established peace, and others were worried that it wouldn't. Toronto saw a huge amount of sympathy extended to the Winnipeg strikers, and labour organizers rallied workers for a general strike on May 30. They managed to close 230 factories and 50 stores but, in their efforts to keep the protest peaceful, the organizers set up regulations over who could strike and who couldn't. The exclusions leeched much of the power of the strike.

However, 2,200 workers at the Toronto Railway Company took advantage of the climate of protest and staged their own strike for better wages. It lasted from June 22 to July 4, when they settled with their employers for a 60 percent pay hike. While the protest continued, cars, trucks and bicycles clogged city streets. Resourceful individuals, taking advantage of the desperate need for transportation, operated jitneys — independently run cars or trucks that crammed passengers inside, charging a fare for each person.

▼ **Visitors to Sunnyside relax on the grass and stroll along the famous boardwalk, 1920s.** The two-mile boardwalk at Sunnyside held its own appeal, not only for the fashionistas who donned their best to stroll its length each Easter Sunday, but also for lovers, families and even city officials. When a pragmatist suggested paving it over to save money, the parks commissioner (whose name, appropriately, was Walter Love) declared that it must remain made of wood. Cement would take away the romance of the lakeside sidewalk.

▶ **Dubbed the "Poor Man's Riviera," the "Lakeside Playground" and the "City of Light," Sunnyside was the classic amusement park** that put the others out of business, combining location, architecture, ambience and a cheap and cheerful midway. Planning began in 1909, but was interrupted by the war. It finally opened in 1922, after a major reclamation of land from the lake. The 130 acres of beach, rides and boardwalk offered a magnet to Torontonians for about 30 years. The Toronto Transportation Commission ran free "bathing cars" to transport kids to the beach, where they could swim in the lake or the Sunnyside Pool. Bathers changed their clothes at the Sunnyside Bathing Pavilion, a Mediterranean palace that sported multiple arches, a tea garden, a terrace and courtyards. The midway was as grubby and tantalizing as a midway should be, with palmistry, games of chance and skill, shooting galleries, a Ferris wheel and a roller coaster. The bandstand, the boardwalk and the swimming pool all helped make it the favourite summer destination for many Torontonians.

▲ **The Sunnyside Pavilion, June 1922, the year it opened.** The elegant bathing pavilion was a welcome addition to Sunnyside Beach. The year before it opened more than 300,000 swimmers enjoyed the beach without benefit of lockers, showers or tea on the terrace. The pavilion provided all these amenities, as well as an atmosphere of glamour and romance. With its Italianate arches and colonnades, open courtyards and upstairs terrace, the Sunnyside Pavilion brought a taste of Mediterranean ease and elegance to the shores of chilly Lake Ontario. When you were inside the courtyards, the view of lake and beach was framed by the graceful row of arches. The tea garden on the upper storey offered a cool spot for refuelling. Downstairs you could rent a locker — there were 7,700 of them — along with soap, towel, a shower and even a swimsuit.

▶ **Cars proceed slowly along Lakeshore Boulevard past Sunnyside Amusement Park, April 1925.** From early spring until fall each year, a bottleneck of traffic blocked the lakeshore at Sunnyside. The park drew thousands to its many diversions, beginning with the often-freezing Easter Parade of fashions along the boardwalk. As the weather warmed up, visitors enjoyed fairground rides and swimming from the elegant Bathing Pavilion. By the late forties Sunnyside's glory days were over. With rumours of an expanded highway along the lake and the demise of the park, the grounds became rundown and attendance began to drop. More people had cars, which meant they could drive farther for their fun. A series of fires prompted the Toronto Harbour Commission to demolish the park in 1955–56, leaving only the Bathing Pavilion and the Palais Royale dancehall as ghostly reminders of the classic amusement park.

◄ **The double Ferris wheels at the Canadian National Exhibition sparkle in the night.** The CNE, just down the lake from Sunnyside, did not offer serious competition to the amusement park, since the Ex was open for only a few weeks toward the end of the summer. Also, the CNE provided a different type of diversion. Along with its thriving midway, it offered grandstand shows and a multitude of exhibits, many of which featured new technology.

▲ **Fred Beasely, known as "Canada's Strongman," lifts three women at Hanlan's Point, Toronto Island, 1922.** Before the advent of Sunnyside Amusement Park in 1922 and Maple Leaf Stadium in 1926, Hanlan's Point Amusement Park drew the crowds, who came by ferry to have fun by the lake. There was a baseball stadium (where Babe Ruth hit his first professional home run, in 1914), an amusement park, a hotel and a beach. The only serious competition was the Scarboro Beach Amusement Park, at the other end of town.

◄ **Bathers swim in the Sunnyside swimming pool and gather on the beach, July 1926.** The Sunnyside "tank" (officially an "outdoor natatorium") opened in 1925, after two cold summers kept swimmers away from the beach. At that time it held the title of largest outdoor pool in the world: 300 feet long and 75 feet wide, filled with 750,000 gallons of water. To bathe in the heated water (maintained at 20°C), adults paid 35 cents and children a dime.

◄ **The first Miss Toronto and runners-up at Sunnyside, 1926.** The first beauty contest for Miss Toronto took place at Sunnyside in August 1926. The traditional wool flannel bathing suits revealed as much of these women's bodies as was acceptable at the time, and the contestants' figures highlight the fact that, despite the flat-chested "flapper" look of the twenties, the ideal of beauty involved more weight than it does now. With her crown of flowers and her winner's wreath hung around her neck, the winner, Miss Jean Ford, smiles beatifically at the crowd.

► **Four women model their fashionable coats and hats at the annual Sunnyside Easter Parade along the boardwalk, April 1936.** Fashions of the thirties were a bit more forgiving for the female figure than the short, dropped-waist skirts of the twenties, which best suited a boyish form. Hemlines fell to mid-calf, the waistline returned to the waist, and saucy hats were designed to frame more abundant tresses. These women are participating in a Toronto ritual: the Easter Parade. No matter what the weather, people donned their finest clothes to brave the windy boardwalk, showing off their new clothes and greeting friends.

► **Two small contestants in the Sunnyside Charleston contest kick up their heels, July 1926.** Attractions at Sunnyside included not only concerts and sports, but also contests — some of them decidedly odd. In 1927 female impersonators participated in their own contest. The same year, kids with freckles and red hair competed to see who was most freckled and reddest-headed. The best dishwasher was selected in a 1934 dishwashing contest.

◀ **On the beach at Hanlan's Point, 1922.** In the twenties, wool was the material of choice for bathing attire. Women wore wool shifts with matching shorts, and men wore a similar costume, sometimes with the kind of cotton singlet sported by the man who is holding the little girl's hand. Beach fashion had come a long way since before the war, when voluminous outfits, especially for women, disguised the natural curves of the body as much as possible. And more daring outfits were on their way.

In July 1936, Torontonians were suffering from one of the worst heat waves in the city's history. Temperatures reached a stifling 40.6°C (105°F) — and these were the days before widespread air-conditioning. In desperation, people left their homes at night to sleep on the grass by the lake at Sunnyside and the CNE grounds. The extreme temperature affected Ontario and Manitoba, with a total of 1,180 deaths attributed to the heat. Newspapers began printing casualty lists each day, as in wartime, because there were too many victims for individual stories to be written. The proverbial eggs were fried on the steps of City Hall, and the city sweltered for 12 days until the heat finally broke.

At the height of the heat wave, 30 men on the beach at Sunnyside rebelled against the Puritan social mores and removed the tops of their bathing suits. In fine Canadian style they were immediately arrested and charged with indecent exposure. They were not convicted and, from then on, it was acceptable for men to go topless on Toronto beaches.

▲ **A woman and two girls wave goodbye to passengers on the lake steamer** *Cayuga,* **Toronto Harbour, circa 1919.** The 305-foot *Cayuga,* launched in 1906 at a cost of $200,000, carried passengers on the Great Lakes for 44 years.

▶ **People wait to board the ferry** *Dalhousie City* **at the Yonge Street Wharf, June 1925.** This passenger ship, along with others operated by the Niagara, St. Catharines and Toronto Navigation Company, ran excursions across Lake Ontario. A favourite destination was Lakeside Park, an amusement park in Port Dalhousie (which has now been absorbed by St. Catharines). At

Lakeside, tourists could catch the radial railway (high-speed electric streetcars) to Niagara Falls.

The popularity of this type of outing can be judged by the summer schedule: four ships made the two-and-a-half-hour trip Monday to Saturday, and three sailed every Sunday.

◀ **Two men are dwarfed by a huge pipe and reservoir that form part of the city's water system, 1922.** Toronto's population grew from 86,000 in 1883 to 521,000 in 1921; and, in 1920, Toronto's water consumption rose to more than 24 billion imperial gallons. Water and sewage systems were forced to keep pace with the expanding city. However, in the late 19th and early 20th centuries, the quality of Toronto's water was a problem that just didn't go away. Providing Toronto with clean water proved extremely tricky, because Lake Ontario served as both the source of water and the ultimate destination of sewage. As the lake became more polluted, the Department of Works had to use longer intake pipes to reach farther into the lake to access cleaner water. The pipes were half a mile long in 1898, a mile in 1905, and a mile and a half in the early 1930s.

By 1913, after years of political wrangling, Toronto finally had a trunk sewer and a sewage treatment and filtration plant. In 1910 chlorinated water was introduced to fight typhoid, and the success of the program made Toronto a leader in the field. Still, people remained suspicious of the chlorine, and in 1927 the city laboratories undertook hourly taste and odour tests. Since the opening in the thirties of the R.C. Harris Filtration Plant in the Beaches, the city has carried out thousands of annual chemical, bacteriological and raw-water tests.

The indoor toilet, prosaic in the extreme, held an important place in the development and function of Toronto as a modern city. In 1912 there were 18,000 outdoor privies in Toronto. Thirteen years later, in 1925, there were only 335. This dramatic reduction was due in part to a 1913 bylaw that allowed the city to install indoor plumbing in people's houses and then add the cost to the individual's tax bill. Connecting all Toronto homes to the sewer system became a priority because of the proliferation of "filth diseases": typhoid, cholera and diphtheria, all of which were associated with outdoor privies and untreated waste. The subsoil seepage

▲ Prince Edward Viaduct under construction, July 1917. Along with the creation of the Toronto Transportation Commission three years later, the Prince Edward Viaduct contributed to the modernization and growth of postwar Toronto by moving traffic and people more efficiently. Originally named the Bloor Viaduct, the mile-long (1.6 km)

contaminated water, the proliferation of flies caused the spread of disease and the smell produced by 18,000 privies can only be imagined. Charles Hastings, the medical officer of health for Toronto, called them the "relics of barbarism."

bridge was renamed in 1919 in honour of the popular Prince of Wales, who presided at the official opening.

The construction of a bridge to connect Danforth Avenue to Bloor Street had been talked about since 1880, though no action was taken until a referendum in the 1913 civic election approved the project. The Public Works Department proceeded with the construction, under the direction of Toronto's commisioner of public works, R.C. Harris. The bridge, built in three sections, opened up the area east of Broadview Avenue by connecting it to downtown. Before 1919, people had to descend into the Don Valley and cross

the river at the Winchester Street Bridge.

Rowland Caldwell Harris presided over the Public Works Department from 1912 to 1945. The Prince Edward Viaduct and the R.C. Harris Filtration Plant in the Beaches are the two most famous of his achievements, but his influence was felt in many other projects throughout the city. Under his direction, roads were widened and paved, uniform street lighting was introduced, and the number of sidewalks in Toronto was doubled. The construction of the viaduct is a famous example of his foresight: Harris ensured that the structure would be strong enough to accommodate a future subway line.

◄ **Blimp flying over Toronto, late 1920s.** At this time the dirigible, or airship, was considered a viable alternative to the airplane. The first successful flight of a steerable dirigible had been achieved by Ferdinand Zeppelin in Germany in 1900. Deployed for surveillance and bombing raids in the Great War, dirigibles were developed for passenger flight and flown in the twenties and thirties. The technical problems involved in flying a huge balloon filled with hydrogen or helium proved daunting. Spectacular crashes — including the tragic end of the English R101 in France in 1931 and the *Hindenberg* disaster over New Jersey in 1937 — sealed the dirigible's fate.

The most famous appearance of a blimp in Toronto was the flyover of the British R100 on August 11, 1930. The R100 and the doomed R101 were both built in Britain, one by a private company and one by the British government. Known respectively as the "capitalist airship" and the "socialist airship," they incorporated the latest technology and were destined for an England-to-Egypt route (the "capitalist" R100) and an England-to-India route (the "socialist" R101). At this time people believed the airship embodied the future of flight, and these two models represented a huge financial investment. The completed R100 was almost 700 feet long with a diameter of about 130 feet; its 15 gas bags held more than 5 million cubic feet of hydrogen gas. Powered by 12 Rolls-Royce 12-cylinder aircraft engines, the dirigible could fly at a maximum speed of about 80 miles per hour.

For a demonstration flight, arrangements were made for the R100 to fly across the Atlantic Ocean to Canada. A special mooring mast had to be built in St. Hubert, Quebec. The blimp set off from England on July 29 and, 78 hours and 49 minutes later, reached St. Hubert. On the following Sunday evening it left Ottawa at 6:17 to make a flight over Toronto and Niagara Falls. Thousands of people gathered on roofs, in parks and along the waterfront to observe it on Monday morning. It flew over downtown just after 9 a.m. Giant letters painted on the City Hall driveway spelled out "Welcome." Then the airship, dubbed the "Silver Ghost" by the *Toronto Telegram,* sailed serenely out of sight on its trip back to Ottawa. The crowds dispersed, but for many the occasion of the R100's flight over Toronto remained a significant memory.

▲ **Looking north on James Street from Queen, circa 1920.** With City Hall barely visible on the left, this photo shows a typical busy day downtown. Eaton's Furniture Building, on the left, later evolved into the "Eaton's Annex." On the right is the Eaton's main store and Adams' Furniture. The intersection of Yonge and Queen streets was dominated by the two rival department stores, Eaton's and Simpsons. Simpsons had a reputation as a slightly more upscale shopping destination, but Eaton's was the more famous: the Queen Street store had everything — clothes, shoes, hardware, furniture, toys, dishes, groceries — plus excellent service. There was a wig-cleaning and shaping service, wheelchairs for customers who needed them, guides for the blind and a shopping service that provided advice on purchasing clothes, gifts, party supplies — or anything else. Customers could buy gifts at Eaton's and have them sent anywhere in the country. There was an optical department, a photo department, an interior decorating department and a candy factory. Wealthy patrons could drop off fur pelts and have them made up into coats.

Staunchly upholding Timothy Eaton's tried-and-true slogans, "The Greatest Good to the Greatest Number of People" and "Goods Satisfactory or Money Refunded," the Eaton's phenomenon had spread to 47 stores across Canada by 1931. Eaton's catalogue service had been thriving for years, bringing goods and equipment to the most far-flung farm or settlement in the country.

◄▼ Eaton's Santa Claus Parade, 1926.
By 1926 the Eaton's Santa Claus Parade was an eagerly anticipated event that drew children out in droves in late November to see the fanfare surrounding Santa's arrival in Toronto. In the 1920s, radio station CFRB broadcast weekly reports that dramatized Santa's adventures on his trip from the North Pole. The excitement built throughout the month until the great day arrived when he appeared at the end of his spectacular parade and made his stately way to Eaton's Queen Street store.

For the first parade, in 1905, Santa arrived in town by train at the old Union Station. In the years that followed he chose many other forms of transportation, including a chariot, a plane and a large silver fish. In 1913 his sleigh was pulled by four reindeer shipped in for the event from the Grenfell Mission in Labrador. Often there were two Santas, one to ride in the float and a spare in a car with darkened windows behind, in case of emergencies. One year rumour had it that Jack Eaton himself played Santa, although he usually rode at the front of the parade in one of his cherished automobiles.

Eaton's paid for the entire parade, including Santa's transport, the costumes and the floats.

▶ The Robert Simpson Company store decorated for the royal visit in May 1939. In the months leading up to the visit of King George VI and Queen Elizabeth, Torontonians entered into a frenzy of beautification and decoration. At the tail end of the Depression, with war imminent in Europe, Canadians needed cheering up. The excitement and fervour aroused by the royal visit engulfed the country. The occasion was historic: King George VI was the first reigning monarch to visit Canada, and the royal couple's progress across the country in their special blue and silver train created a thrilling spectacle for thousands of Canadians.

In Toronto, a "Beautify Toronto for the Royal Visit" campaign urged citizens to tidy up their front yards, plant flowers and paint their houses in anticipation of the royals' visit. Even though the visiting couple would not be seeing most of the houses, Torontonians enthusiastically beautified their properties. On the actual parade routes, stores hung out banners, ribbons and other decorations, along with dozens of Union Jacks. And on the corner of its store, Simpsons mounted a huge statue of the king, topped by an enormous crown.

▲ **Streetcars, cars and a Gray Coach bus travel west along Front Street between Bay and York, circa 1930.** The Toronto Transportation Commission took over Gray Coach Lines in 1927 to carry passengers to towns and cities in Ontario and New York State.

At the very beginning of the 1920s Toronto's transportation systems were overhauled by the newly formed Toronto Transportation Commission (TTC), which created a modern, integrated system that drew the city together. Toronto is still reaping the benefits of the high standards set then.

When it took over city transit in 1921, the TTC faced a formidable challenge. The city had been held hostage for 30 years by the Toronto Railway Company (TRC), headed by businessman William Mackenzie. The TRC

negotiated a 30-year franchise in 1891 and refused to expand its original routes or services, even though the city grew far beyond the boundaries in the agreement. Other railway companies formed to extend the service, but passengers had to pay separate fares and endure long lineups at the transfer points. For much of TRC's reign, the company was involved in litigation with the City of Toronto, which tried to force the TRC to improve service or else give up the franchise. In 1907 the battle went all the way to the Privy Council in London, England, at that time the last court of appeal for Canadian disputes. The Privy Council voted in favour of the TRC's retaining its franchise, and Toronto had to put up with a poor transit system for another 14 years.

On January 2, 1920, Toronto citizens voted

in a referendum to run the transit system as a public enterprise. The TTC inherited a mess: all the streetcar lines that served Toronto added up to nine different branches of rail systems. The lack of efficient, affordable transportation had slowed the city's development, both commercially and residentially. People just couldn't get around.

The tracks needed repairing, replacing and extending; the streetcars needed to be refurbished or replaced; and the intersections needed to be rebuilt with new tracks. The TTC rose beautifully to the challenge and laid the foundation for the transit system the city enjoys today — one of the most respected in North America. The company did it with grace and style: there were no major disruptions of service or traffic, and intersections were often rebuilt overnight. In the first few

years the TTC built 43 miles of new track, rebuilt 67 miles of damaged track, and repaired 42 miles of old track. The company bought 575 new Peter Witt steel streetcars and added buses to the less-travelled routes that didn't warrant streetcar tracks. It spent nearly $50 million in the first year, most of which was provided by the city. With a fare of 25 cents for four tickets, the TTC eventually paid back its debt and became self-sufficient.

The benefits of an efficient transportation system cannot be overestimated. It confirmed Toronto's status as a modern city. Thanks to low fares and widespread accessibility, people not only could work in a part of the city away from where they lived, but also could easily gather for social activities or political rallies. The development

of the city itself was given a tremendous boost. Subdivisions that were under-developed before 1920 could now be built up, since houses would sell to buyers who could get to work on the streetcar without difficult transfers, high fares and endless lineups. "Streetcar strips" appeared along Eglinton, Bayview and the Danforth, with shops on the ground floor and apartments above. People took the streetcar to Sunnyside, the Canadian National Exhibition, the ferry docks and the Beaches.

The system was known as one of the best in North America. The TTC boasted that 87.5 percent of Torontonians lived within a thousand feet of services and 99.6 percent lived within two thousand feet. In 1934 an efficiency expert gave the system a glowing review:

"There is no comparable system where the entire personnel appears to be working so harmoniously to the one end of furnishing the best possible transportation service in the most economical manner . . . none with records and data so complete . . . none in better physical condition . . . none with lower fares; under comparable conditions . . . none with higher average speeds or with better frequency of service . . . none with a better safety record."

▲ Spadina Avenue was so wide that these cars could park at right angles to the sidewalk, late 1930s.

◄ **Looking north along Yonge Street, with Adelaide Street in the foreground, circa 1930.** The Union Jacks hung out across the street suggest a holiday or an upcoming parade or patriotic occasion. Note two businesses that would later move uptown: Holt Renfrew and Ryrie Birks (Birks's predecessor).

▲ **Children en route to play school, 1929.**
Local settlement houses organized play
schools for preschool children from
underprivileged families. The children
played games, sang songs and enjoyed a
milk-and-biscuit break.

Christian settlement houses came into
being as the result of a reform movement
in the Presbyterian Church in Britain, the
United States and Canada. They were
established in downtown neighbourhoods,
where large numbers of immigrants and
working people lived. The larger purpose of
the houses was to encourage social harmony
through education and example, with a

strong dose of Christian evangelical mission.
The Canadianization of immigrants (teaching them British values and customs) was
part of the philosophy.

Staff members lived in the settlement
houses, becoming part of the neighbourhood while devoting their time to social
work. They focused their attention on
providing education and health care,
especially to children, and their mandate
addressed issues of illness, poverty, cruelty,
child labour and delinquency.

Toronto at this time had several settlement houses, including St. Christopher
House near Kensington Market; Central

Neighbourhood House in the Ward; and the
University Settlement House. The houses
offered mothers and children a centre where
the kids would be looked after while the
moms joined clubs or attended lectures on
homemaking and childcare. Mothers were
encouraged to take their babies to the well-
baby clinics. There were also numerous
classes and clubs for children and men (all
run on the democratic principle) — English
language, Bible study, crafts and drama, as
well as summer camps outside the city.
Juvenile delinquents were encouraged to
join Scouts and baseball, hockey and
basketball teams.

▶ **A baby being weighed at the baby clinic at Central Neighbourhood House while mothers wait their turn and a volunteer updates records, 1929.** The introduction of well-baby clinics and milk depots during the first decades of the 20th century played an important part in improving public health in the city. With modernization, urban growth, improved water and sewer systems and an aggressive public health campaign came a dramatic decrease in the communicable diseases that cut a swath through the population in the late 19th century.

Tuberculosis, the big killer, fell from 130 deaths per 100,000 in 1910 to fewer than 30 in 1940. Death rates for diphtheria, typhoid and smallpox were also greatly reduced.

Well-baby clinics were a fixture by the 1920s, spread through the downtown area where the population was most dense. In settlement houses and missions, doctors and nurses held sessions for mothers and their new babies. The infants were weighed, careful records were kept of each child's progress, and mothers received advice on how to improve or maintain their children's health. The public health nurses also gave advice on breastfeeding and the general care of the baby, including bathing, while volunteers provided snacks and helped with the ongoing work of the clinic. Milk depots provided safe, pasteurized milk for mothers who couldn't afford it.

The success and proliferation of the well-baby clinics were a direct result of a shocking report in 1910, which revealed that 131 babies out of every 1,000 born in Toronto died before the age of one. The causes were put down to poverty and the mothers' lack of knowledge of sanitation and proper feeding techniques. Many of the babies died as a result of diarrheal disease.

The Department of Health initiated a campaign to educate women and provide medical advice through the baby clinics. Public health nurses acted as both educators and social workers, carrying out home visits to teach women how to care for their babies. The nurses also offered practical advice about cleanliness — how to keep flies out of the house, for example — and refrigeration. Three multilingual nurses were hired to communicate with non-English-speaking immigrants from Italy, Poland, Russia and Macedonia.

By 1923 the infant mortality rate had dropped by 50 percent to 63 per 1,000. By 1924, 75 percent of mothers in Toronto were breastfeeding their children. And in 1928 1,667 clinic sessions were held in the city and 47,096 children were examined by doctors or nurses. Improved nutrition, sanitation, housing and sewer systems all were factors in the drop in the mortality rate, but the success of the well-baby clinic was near the top of the list.

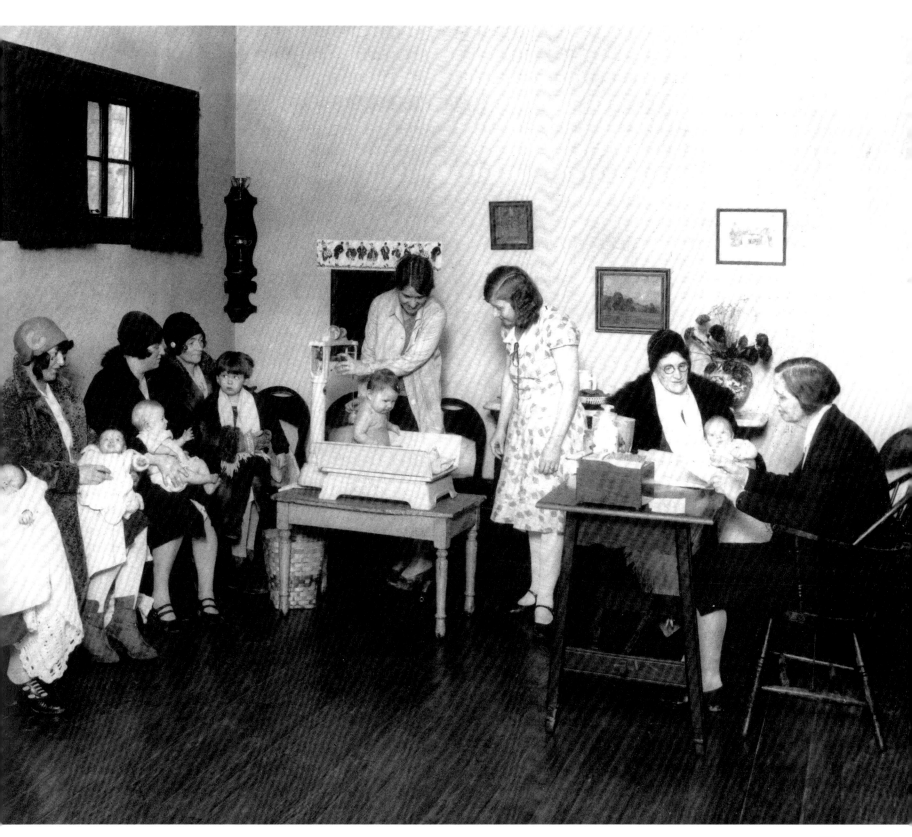

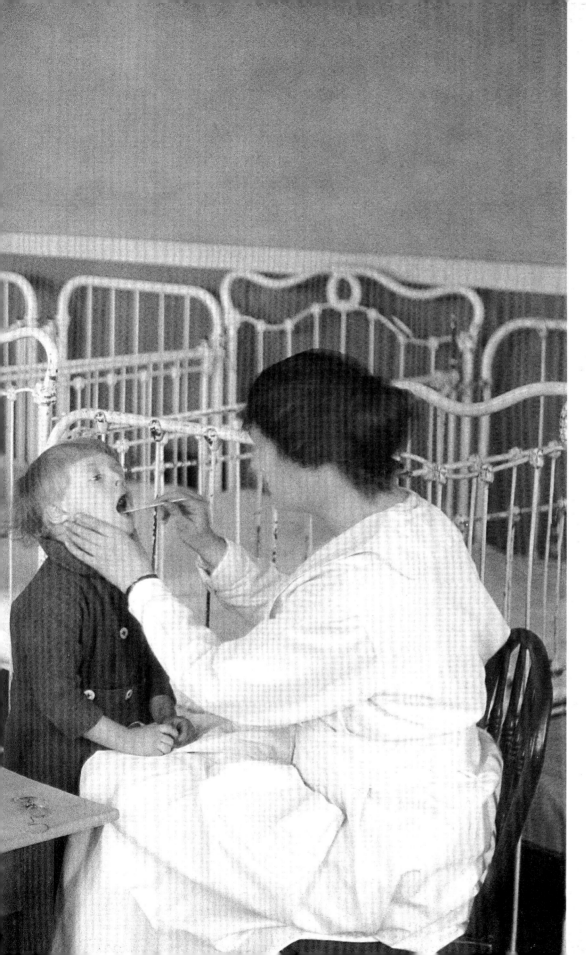

◀ **Children line up apprehensively to have their throats checked by a nurse at the Creche Day Nursery on Euclid Avenue, February 1923.** These preschoolers were fortunate to receive individual care in the middle of flu season. Health care providers and educators had known for quite some time that attention to children's health before they reached kindergarten age was critical. In the late 19th century, children whose families could not afford regular medical checkups lacked proper care. But with the sweeping health care reforms of the early 20th century, that changed.

At first the well-baby clinics were only for children under the age of one. But as the clinics proved successful, they developed into child health centres where mothers could bring their preschool children, as well as their babies, for regular checkups. By 1922, 21 clinics across the city provided free health care for children.

Many doctors opposed these clinics. Most physicians approved in principle the idea that people who couldn't afford their fees should have access to free medical care, but they objected to losing their paying customers. However, strong public support and improved child care during the twenties and thirties ensured that the clinics stayed open, although services were reduced during the Depression.

▲ **People line up outside the Mutual Street Arena for the first service held by the newly formed United Church of Canada, June 10, 1925.** The inaugural service of the United Church of Canada marked the end of years of negotiations for union among the Presbyterian, Methodist and Congregationalist churches in Canada.

In the first decades of the 20th century, established religion played a much greater role in Toronto society than it does today.

Toronto churches were filled for two services a day, with the major denominations represented in most neighbourhoods. In 1921 Anglicans were in the majority (33 percent), followed by Presbyterians (21 percent), Methodists (16 percent) and Catholics (12 percent).

The road toward church union was an arduous one, causing disputes between family members and within congregations. In the end, some Congregational churches

voted against union and about one-third of Presbyterians chose to remain independent. But the others drew together to form what was very nearly a national church. The participants in the union believed that a country as widespread as Canada needed a strong church to reach as many citizens as possible. One of the interesting progressive features of the United Church was the ordination of women, which was approved in 1936.

By 1930 the United Church congregations formed the second largest religious group in Toronto (21 percent), with the Anglicans retaining their majority (31 percent). On a secular level, the formation of the United Church could be seen as one in the eye for the hoity-toity Anglicans who, for over a hundred years, had enjoyed their position as the dominant church in Toronto — with all the influence in government and society that it entailed.

▲ **Children at a play-school Christmas party at Central Neighbourhood House, 1929.** Unlike most of the settlement houses in Toronto, this one — in the poorest and most needy area — did not have a direct connection to a Protestant church. Staff members provided services to the immigrant population, doing their best to respect the ethnic identity of their clients while helping them to adjust to life in Toronto. They helped residents of the Ward deal with landlords, work with city officials and tackle the multitude of other problems that they faced. Children received presents and refreshments at the annual Christmas parties.

◀ **A group of unemployed men sleep on newspapers in the bandshell at Queen's Park, 1938.** Although the worst of the Depression had passed by this point, many of Toronto's citizens still experienced suffering and deprivation. Work remained scarce until the country started gearing up for the Second World War.

▲ **Unemployed men riding the rails, 1935.** For far too many Canadians in the thirties, the transient life seemed the only way to survive. Hoping to find work of some kind, men took to riding the rails from city to city. Because Toronto was a little better off than other places, people poured in — stretching the city's resources to the limit. Between 1931 and 1936, more than half of the men registered for relief were transients.

They lined up at soup kitchens and slept wherever they could: on the streets and in tarpaper shacks, garbage dumps, underground burrows and parks. The historic St. Lawrence Hall was converted to a flophouse with the addition of steel bunks. All day the men wandered the streets, looking for work or handouts. They adopted the traditional tramp's chalk symbols to mark which houses were more generous.

▲ **Worried customers gather outside the Bloor and Bathurst branch of the Dominion Bank during a run on the bank, October 1923.** These people were hoping to withdraw their money, fearful that the bank would fail and they would lose everything. This run on the Dominion Bank was caused by an atmosphere of distrust set off by the failure of the Home Bank. On an August morning that year, the Home Bank's doors were locked and its business suspended. It was then that its depositors had their first inkling that they were in danger of losing their savings. Their worst fears were realized when it became clear in the following few days that the Home Bank had made huge unsecured loans and its assets were insufficient to cover them. All the investors in the bank lost their money. Forty-seven of the 71 branches in Canada were in Ontario, and most depositors were Catholics or Catholic institutions, including school boards, the Knights of Columbus and parish churches.

At the June annual meeting, the bank's business was presented as above-board and successful. But the general manager died in the first week of August. His assistant took over and blew the whistle on a disgraceful situation of bad debts and deception. The directors of the bank had made wildly extravagant loans — $6 million worth — to companies in which they had interests. The

Canadian Bankers' Association refused to help, and the bank collapsed.

On October 3, the key players were all arrested: the directors and the president, vice-president, chief accountant and chief auditor. It was in this climate of panic and loss of faith that the run on the Dominion Bank began 10 days later. Depositors clamoured for their money. This time the Ontario government stepped in and made a deposit of $1.5 million. Premier George Howard Ferguson gave a speech to calm the public.

Ultimately the failure of the Home Bank brought about some much-needed changes in the banking system. The federal government introduced banking legislation and created an inspector general of banks to ensure that this kind of fiasco would never happen again. A year after the bank's failure, the citizens of Toronto were treated to a sensational five-month trial of the bank officers and directors. Although the directors were at first found guilty, their convictions were later overturned. Two of the players were dead: the general manager at the outset of the crisis, and the president the following June. Many ordinary citizens saw their savings wiped out, and some rich bank patrons who had borrowed heavily from the Home Bank were ruined, among them Sir Henry Pellatt.

◄ An evicted man sits with his possessions on the street, circa 1919. Evictions during the twenties and thirties were all too common. Like this unfortunate man in the hard times just after the war, people who couldn't pay their rent were turfed out of their houses with all their goods. During the Depression it only got worse, but in the politically charged climate of the thirties neighbours often rallied around to try to stop an eviction. Word spread as soon as the news of an upcoming eviction hit the street. Enterprising activists mimeographed and circulated thousands of leaflets, and crowds of up to a thousand would show up at a house to prevent city officials from doing their jobs. Sometimes the police would be called in to use strong-arm tactics and make arrests. Although some evictions were delayed, unless money could be raised the family was eventually put out on the street.

► Children in a poor neighbour-hood, circa 1930.

◄ **Marchers in the Toronto version of the On to Ottawa Trek, July 1935.** On July 17, 1935, 300 walkers sponsored by the National Unemployment Council started their trek from Toronto to Ottawa. This was a much smaller version of the On to Ottawa Trek that began in Vancouver in June 1935 and cnded in Regina on July 1 with one of the worst riots in Canadian history. The trek came after weeks of strike action in Vancouver by the highly organized National Unemployed Workers Association, which grew out of the relief camps in British Columbia. Following demonstrations, sit-ins and much public support, the trek was organized to publicize the cause of unemployed workers and to get some action from the federal government. The idea was that the men would ride the rails and go to Ottawa to demand wages and work.

The trek embodied the frustration felt by unemployed workers across the country. Everywhere the men stopped, people provided them with food and moral support. The participants were carefully supervised. There were no difficulties until the federal government finally responded — and called a halt in Regina by instructing the railway not to let the men back on the trains. A delegation of their representatives met the prime minister in Ottawa. The meeting came to nothing but angry recriminations on both sides, and the leaders returned to Regina to call off the trek.

The police moved in to break up a final public meeting in downtown Regina, and a terrible riot resulted. Police beat the demonstrators unmercifully with wooden clubs, and the demonstrators fought back with whatever they could lay their hands on. Bullets were fired, one policeman died from his injuries, dozens were wounded and 130 trekkers were arrested. The trek was over. However, this smaller contingent set out from Toronto on July 17 and reached Ottawa 22 days later. The prime minister scolded them for 15 minutes.

◀ **A lineup at a soup kitchen, 1934.**
In 1933, 30 percent of employable
Torontonians were jobless. Because of a
diversified economy that was based on
farming, manufacturing and the mining
centres of Northern Ontario, Toronto
during the Depression suffered less than
other parts of Canada. Still, the level
of deprivation in the city wore people
down. By 1934, when this photograph
was taken, 120,000 unemployed
Torontonians were on relief. People lost
their savings, their houses and their
dreams for the future. Companies cut
down on hours and wages. Workers had
to adjust and somehow get by. Often
families doubled up in houses or
apartments to save on rent.

The government was slow to respond
to the needs of the homeless and the
jobless. The Toronto House of Industry,
which was basically a poorhouse,
began to supply food packages to needy
families. By 1933 the Department of
Welfare had developed a system that
allowed people to use vouchers for
food and clothing at cooperating stores
throughout the city. Human nature being
what it is, some people who were not
entitled tried to take advantage of the
system; and others, who were starving,
were too proud to apply for assistance.

The costs to the city government
were astronomical, even with the federal
government and the province each
donating a third of the total relief bill.
The worst year was 1935, when the city
paid $10 million for relief. By the end
of the decade, Toronto had spent $61.3
million on relief, $14.9 million of which
was borrowed.

► **Commissioner and Mrs. David C. Lamb of the Salvation Army, England, at the Immanuel Baptist Church in Toronto on September 29, 1925**. More than 250 women who had settled in Canada, most of them with the help of the Salvation Army, turned out to honour the visiting couple with a "Hallelujah Reception." The Salvation Army, founded in 1878 by an English evangelist, William Booth, was a fast-growing religious and social-service movement that first came to Toronto in 1882. Its mission was to reach people who wouldn't go to church, and the "army" initially arranged open-air meetings in the slums of London. Organized along military lines with officers, flags and bands, it fought a war for the souls of the downtrodden. An early phrase associated with its work, "Soup to Salvation," described its basic philosophy of caring for physical needs before spiritual ones. At first the Salvation Army found acceptance difficult in mainstream Canada, and its members were sometimes beaten or jailed. But the organization eventually won respect for its social work: providing homes for prisoners leaving jail, creating shelters for the homeless, assisting immigrants, organizing programs for soldiers and their families, and eventually establishing maternity homes and hospitals. During the Depression the Salvation Army, along with the rest of the country, suffered a financial crisis. Donations declined and it struggled to pay its own officers. Its social work declined as a result, but the army rallied and, in the Second World War, contributed to the war effort through its work with the armed forces.

▶ **An enthusiastic crowd of about 40,000 turns out at the annual May Day Parade, 1936.** The participants included choirs, sports associations, trade unions, bands and political groups. During the thirties this traditional labour parade became a rallying point for protesters demonstrating their dissatisfaction with the government in the face of the devastating effects of the Depression. The decade began with a sudden plunge into economic uncertainty and widespread unemployment. It continued with labour unrest, demonstrations, fierce police repression and, finally, a change at City Hall that reflected the widespread discontent of the populace. The social agitation following the war that culminated in the Winnipeg General Strike of 1919 demonstrated what can happen when enough unhappy people join forces. In the thirties, political and labour protest exploded.

The Depression hit the working class the hardest, with massive unemployment and inadequate relief systems. Construction came to a virtual standstill, manufacturing was cut back drastically, and working conditions regressed to the level seen at the turn of the century. Wages in 1933 were at 60 percent of what they had been in 1929. The federal and provincial governments moved very slowly to bring relief, and much of the task was left to the municipalities. Public works were introduced as make-work projects. But it was difficult to fund them, and many people ended up on welfare.

A culture of labour activism grew up in Toronto, much of it localized along Spadina Avenue, where the garment factories provided employment with low wages and long hours. New immigrants, crowded in flats and working in the neighbourhood, joined labour associations in the hope that political action would improve their living and working conditions. A labour organization provided a social context as well and often functioned as a second home for young people. Many of the members of these organizations were Jewish

and, in the bigoted atmosphere of the time, all Jews were accused of being communists and troublemakers. (When the Communist Party of Canada was founded in 1924, statistics told a different story: 50 percent were Finns, 20 percent were Ukrainians and 15 percent were Jews.)

Spadina Avenue was hot with strikes, political speakers on the street corners, interfering policeman, scuffles and arrests. Two general strikes that seemed to involve the entire street — one in 1931 and the other in 1933 — ended with the companies forced to provide minimum wages and better conditions.

An unfortunate development at this time in Toronto was a campaign of repression carried out by the police force, whose members took it upon themselves to suppress any outbreaks of protest. Communism and the violent overthrow of government seemed a very real threat to the police and many others in the troubled atmosphere of the time. Supported by three of the city's newspapers (the *Telegram*, the *Globe,* and the *Mail and Empire*), the police did everything they could to prevent any "suspicious" groups from meeting. When the gatherings took place anyway, the police broke them up with brute force. They even used gas bombs to disrupt meetings, and they threatened to fine landlords who rented halls to labour or protest groups. The police prevented people from gathering at Queen's Park for protest meetings, often beating up protesters and innocent bystanders.

The arrest, trial and imprisonment of eight communist leaders in Toronto in 1931 had repercussions across the country. In Toronto, university professors protested the incursions on free speech and voiced their concerns publicly. Many other citizens gradually realized that the police had gone too far. In 1934 the eight leaders were released, with a huge rally held in Maple Leaf Gardens to welcome them back to the city. And in 1935 Toronto elected a new mayor — Jimmie Simpson, a labour activist. The tide had turned.

Members of the East York Workers Association gather around their CCF banner, May Day Parade, May 1, 1936. The Co-operative Commonwealth Federation had drawn on organized labour for political support since its 1932 founding in Calgary. Farmers' organizations, trade-union supporters, some sympathetic members of Parliament and academics — led by the CCF's founder and first leader, J.S. Woodsworth — drew together to work for social change, the nationalization of industries and a welfare state. Fuelled by the desperate economic climate of the times, the CCF saw its popularity grow rapidly. In 1935, the year before this picture was taken, it elected seven members of Parliament and carried 8.9 percent of the popular vote.

▶ **Shoppers select oranges from a wagon, 1924.** Jews settling in Toronto in the early years of the 20th century had two basic needs: to practise their religious rituals, and to make a living. They developed small businesses such as kosher butcher shops, poultry and fish markets, bakeries, religious book stores, stores selling prayer shawls, dry goods shops and hardware stores. They built synagogues and, in the twenties, founded a kosher hospital, Mount Sinai, at 100 Yorkville Avenue, taking the name from the famous Jewish hospital in New York City.

Before 1920, the majority of Jewish immigrants lived in the infamous Ward, a crowded neighbourhood teeming with life but providing few comforts. It occupied the blocks roughly between Queen Street to the south and College Street to the north, Yonge Street on the east and University Avenue on the west. People lived in cramped quarters. Privies were outside, and sometimes a single water tap supplied an entire block. Because it was cheap to live there, it was a popular spot for new immigrants. By the First World War the area was notably Jewish, with Jewish shops, cafés, a news agency, a seltzer factory, theatres and synagogues. There were factories, many of them notorious for deplorable conditions and low wages. But this area was also the location of the Eaton's factories, which had somewhat better environments and where, in 1911, 80 percent of the workers were Jewish.

As Jewish immigrants gained a foothold and made some money, they started moving out of the Ward to better neighbourhoods west of University. When they settled the Kensington Market area, some opened shops in their houses. To fight the competition from the street vendors, the Jewish merchants began moving their goods onto the sidewalk — and one of Toronto's most colourful neighbourhoods was created. Kensington's small stores, protected from the weather by awnings, lined the narrow streets. Here the street life mimicked an Eastern European *shtetl* (village). It was against the zoning regulations of the time to sell goods on the sidewalk, but the shopkeepers fought for the right to do it, and they eventually won.

And Jews slowly began taking their place in the city's politics. In 1924 Nathan Phillips began his political career when he was elected alderman. He had to join the Conservative party to win. Thirty years later, in 1955, he was elected "mayor of all the people."

In his book *Toronto: The Way It Was*, Michael Kluckner wrote that this move west to Kensington from the Ward was a turning point for the Jewish community. Coming as it did during the First World War, a time of general upheaval throughout the city, it marked a significant change in the status of Jews in Toronto. As the city moved into the twenties, which Kluckner called a period of "considerable liberalism, social change and optimism," the Jews had established themselves as a diverse and settled community. Many worked in the garment factories along Spadina Avenue and, by joining labour organizations, strove to improve their working conditions. Some forward-looking members of the community felt that Kensington was too much like the "old country," while the Orthodox were scandalized at the stores being kept open on Saturday, the Jewish sabbath. The mix of old world and new created a vibrant community that would make a lasting impression on the city.

Kosher butcher shop, probably in
Kensington Market, June 1923.

Woman carrying a hen in
Kensington Market, July 1926.

▲ **Three immigrant boys play with hoops on Chestnut Street in the Ward, August 1922.** Immigrants from many countries came to the Ward as their first stop in the new world. Living conditions were often primitive, but housing was cheap and available, and work plentiful in the neighbourhood's factories, shops and streets. Plans and strategies for cleanup carried over from one decade to the next. Ultimately, the development of the city led to the neighbourhood's demise, with the encroachment in the 1960s of businesses, hospitals and, finally, New City Hall.

▶ **Elderly man loads a baby carriage, Kensington Market, July 1926.**

▲ **Office workers in the accounting department at Loblaws, October 1926.**
The first Loblaws grocery store was opened in Toronto in 1919 by Theodore Pringle Loblaw and Justin Milton Cork. The novel features of cash and carry and self-service meant less staff, lower prices and a wide variety of products. The public loved the concept, and the company expanded to include more stores. By 1934 there were 111 Loblaws throughout Ontario, with the head office and warehouse located at Bathurst Street and Lakeshore Boulevard.

▶ **Women working in the Colgate factory in Toronto's east end, near Dundas Street and Carlaw, 1919.** The First World War changed women's working lives dramatically, as they took over many of the jobs usually performed by men. The end of the war saw a shift back to traditional jobs for women, but the number of women in the workforce gradually increased as they slowly moved into the service sector. In 1921 about 30 percent of working women had jobs in factories, including the garment and textile sweatshops. By 1931 that number was 25 percent, while half the clerical workers were women. Women worked as typists, sales clerks, teachers and telephone operators. The majority of women employees were single, since most companies imposed a rule that, upon marriage, a woman had to give up her job   to become a homemaker. Her husband was expected to provide the family income.

◄ **This Italian resident is sharpening his hand sickle, which he has been using to harvest a field of oats that he planted on Sunnyside Drive, 1924.** During the twenties and thirties, Italians represented the third-largest ethnic group in Toronto, after the British and the Jews. In 1941, 14,000 (or just over 2 percent of the city's population) called Toronto home. The big immigration from Italy came later, in the 1950s.

Despite its relatively modest represent-ation in the city, the Italian community filled the CNE grandstand at its annual summer picnic. The Italians brought their culture with them and, despite all the attempts by British Canadians to assimilate them, remained staunchly Italian.

One of the characteristics of many immigrants to Toronto in the early part of the century — Macedonians and Chinese, as well as Italians — was an attitude that Canada was a temporary home, where you could earn money to send to the old country. Men came on their own and left their wives and families behind. For example, in 1907, 4,500 Italian men entered Canada, but only 400 women accompanied them. The men lived in cramped boarding houses to save as much money as possible. As the years wore on, many of them eventually sent for their families and slowly adapted to life in Canada.

Italian immigrants to Toronto came mostly from Calabria and Sicily in the south and Abruzzi and Lazio in central Italy, although some also originated in the northeast, near Venice and Verona. Many Italian farmers were poor and worked hard for little return; after centuries of over-division of land, no room remained to make a living. Opportunities in Canada were attractive, and the money sent home changed the economic life of the villages back home.

This man has obviously decided to stay in Toronto — putting down roots of the most literal kind by cultivating his city lot to grow food.

▲ **An elderly construction worker uses a pick to break up a huge piece of concrete from the old Custom House on Front Street, 1928.** With the city bustling in the background, the picture focuses on this man's enormous task. Construction work was obviously not for the weak or faint-hearted, and the dangers and hard physical labour involved broke many a man's health. Working conditions could lead to chronic difficulties, injuries and even death — and there was little recourse for social assistance if a man couldn't keep working.

▲ Two boys enjoying the snow in High Park, 1926.

▶ Two days before Christmas, 1925, these children are gathering around the Shriners' Santa at the Empire Theatre. From the perspective of modern-day Toronto, these two pictures show nothing out of the ordinary. But in the Toronto of the twenties and thirties, the black population was tiny. There had been blacks in Toronto since the town of York was first settled in 1793, but in 1931 they numbered only 1,344. Toronto's black population faced various degrees of prejudice and discrimination, although over the years there were notable exceptions of blacks holding positions of authority. William Peyton Hubbard, Toronto's first black alderman, served as councillor, controller and acting mayor of Toronto between 1894 and 1907. His son, Frederick Langton Hubbard, was a transit commissioner and served as general manager of Scarboro Beach Park. A street in the Beaches is named for him.

▶ **People gather on Spadina Avenue outside the Hebrew Men of England synagogue, 1920s.** In 1927 there were about 30 synagogues in the predominantly Jewish neighbourhood west of University Avenue to Bathurst Street between Queen and Bloor streets. Each was built and used by a homogeneous group that originated in a specific part of Europe. There was the Kiever synagogue (still there) on Denison Square, designed by Benjamin Swartz in 1927, and the palatial Goel Tzedic synagogue on Spadina. The synagogue in this picture has a peculiar history. It was built in 1888 by a Congregational church and known as the Western Congregational Church. Designed on a grand scale, it seated 775 people, with galleries around three sides of the interior, a choir platform, and a 37-foot-high ceiling. But by 1920 the congregation wasn't quite big enough to sustain the large building, so its members united with another church and sold this one to the Hebrew Men of England, an Eastern European group of Jews. The architect, Benjamin Swartz, drew up plans to adapt the building to a style more suitable for a synagogue. It became known as "the Londoner Shul," and began its life as a synagogue in August 1922.

By 1920, one-fifth of the population of Toronto was made up of immigrants from all parts of Europe (not including Britain). Of these 100,000 people, the largest group was Jewish, representing about 6 percent of the city's population. The numbers of Jews in Canada grew exponentially in the years between 1901 and 1931, from 3,000 to 45,000. During this time the overall population of the city grew from 156,000 to 631,000.

As in most western countries of the time, anti-Semitism was widespread and all too often tolerated in Canada. Two Toronto publications, the *Telegram* and *Saturday Night,* made their anti-Semitic stance very clear. In the turbulent political climate of the thirties, Jews were blamed for communism, and many Torontonians assumed that all Jews were communists. Although Jews were active in labour organizations, only 15 percent of signed-up communists were Jews when the Communist Party of Canada was founded in 1924.

Most of the Jewish immigrants came to Canada to escape religious persecution in their own countries. Although there were no pogroms in Canada, prejudice was strongly entrenched in the community. Many doors were closed to Jews. Doctors and nurses were not allowed to train at the big hospitals, and summer resorts, hotels, dance halls and many social clubs refused entry to Jews. Signs posted at Toronto's Balmy Beach and Kew Beach read, "No Jews, Niggers or Dogs." Skirmishes broke out between young men who called themselves the "Swastika Club" and young Jews. It all came to a head at a baseball game at Christie Pits in August 1933, when the fans of rival Jewish and anti-Jewish teams erupted into a battle. Mistakenly, the police let it rage for a time and, as a result, the battle grew into a riot involving 10,000 people fighting in the area for more than six hours. Many were badly injured, and there were some arrests.

The Christie Pits riot was the most dramatic outbreak of hatred against Jews in Toronto during the period. Meanwhile, members of the Jewish community were settling into Toronto and making it as livable as possible for themselves. Jewish cultural life took root in Toronto, first in the Ward and then in Kensington Market.

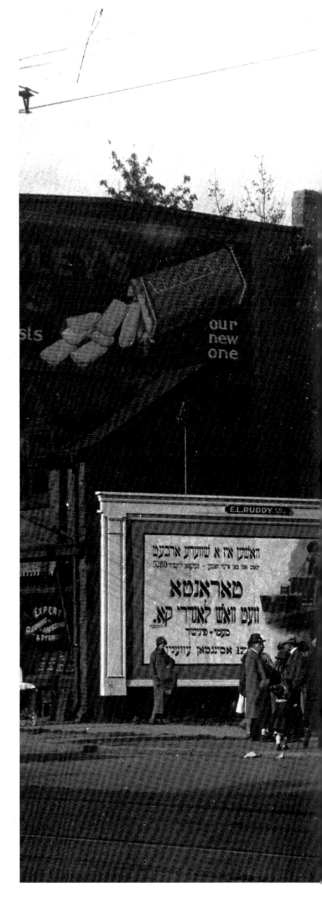

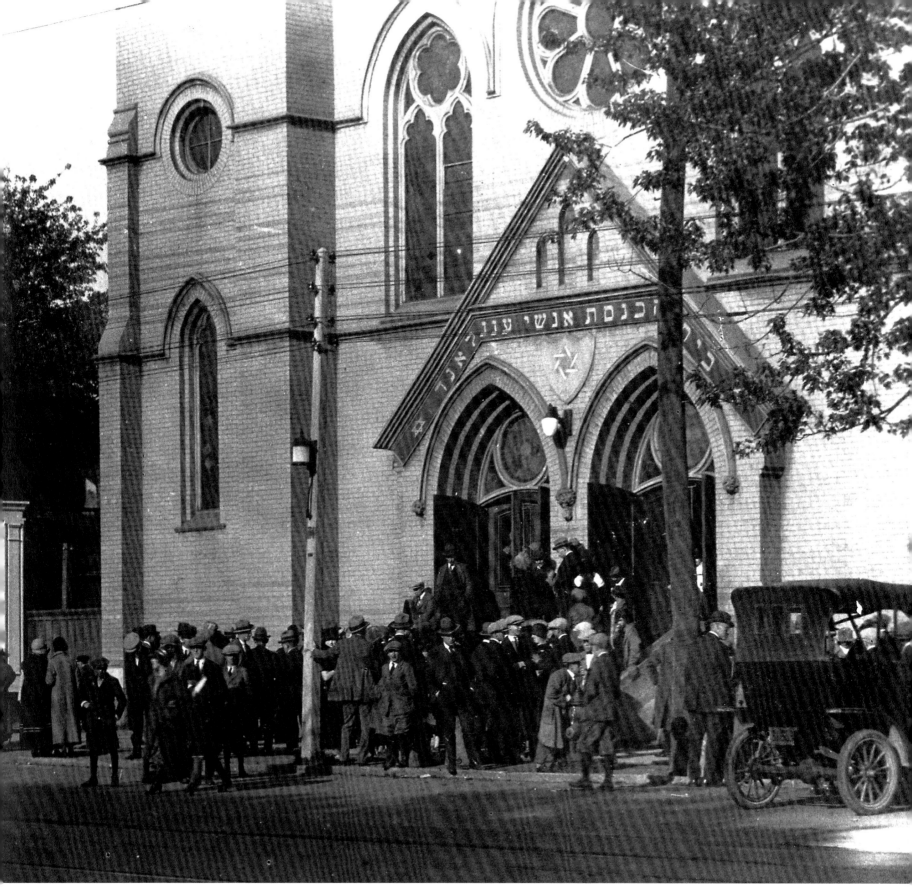

▲ **Chinese children at a picnic, June 1926.**
Their names are written on tags around
their necks.

The Chinese, along with blacks, held
the lowest position in the British hierarchy
of "desirable aliens." They performed the
most menial work and faced discrimination
everywhere. In 1923 the *Chinese Immigration
Act* stopped all Chinese immigration. At the
time, the men far outnumbered the women,
since many were supporting wives and
children in China.

By 1931 only 2,635 Chinese lived in
Toronto. Their main source of employment
remained Chinese restaurants and laundries.
In 1921 the city had 80 Chinese restaurants;
in 1922 there were 370 Chinese laundries.
The restaurants served Chinese and Canadian
food, though their customers were mainly
Canadian. Through the twenties, the Ward
became more of a Chinese neighbourhood
as the Jews and Italians moved west.
Chinatown was concentrated along Dundas
Street between Yonge and University until
the New City Hall was built in the 1960s.

▶ A Jewish mandolin orchestra, 1932.

▼ Gunnar Gustafson's dance orchestra, circa 1930. During the thirties, this group of musicians performed twice a week at the Labour Temple on Spadina Avenue.

▼ **An Italian woman makes tomato paste in her backyard, 1936.** During the very early years of the 20th century, the Ward functioned as the foreign quarter for immigrants coming to Toronto. Situated between Queen and College and Yonge and University, it was increasingly threatened by the development of downtown. The narrow, crowded streets and back alleys overflowed with humanity. Men's boarding houses were popular for those immigrants who didn't see themselves as permanent residents. Beds — as many as could be squeezed into a room — were filled, sometimes 24 hours a day, with men on shiftwork.

Often new immigrants worked as rag-pickers. Some Italians earned a living by taking performing bears around the city's streets. Life was colourful, but uncomfortable. An alternative to working in garment factories or on construction gangs was for an immigrant to save some money to invest in a few goods and start a peddling business. It was hard work to pull a cart all over town, but it paid off. Eventually he could afford a horse, and then perhaps even open a little shop.

Italians who had grown up on farms handling perishable foods naturally gravitated toward the same kind of work in their new city. They woke up before dawn and made their way to the railway sidings to buy fruit wholesale, then set off through the far-flung streets of Toronto to sell it. They were called "banana men" and had almost as big an impact as the transit system in opening up subdivisions. With fresh vegetables and fruit, the new residents could live as well as the people who had easier access to grocery stores downtown. Repairmen and tinkers also made their way to the newly developed areas, bringing commerce along with them.

The Italians started to move west, out of the Ward. In about 1905 Italian grocers

and vegetable stands appeared in the area bounded by Dundas and College and Grace and Manning. As the years passed, more and more Italians moved into the area. Little Italy was well established by the twenties and thirties, a home away from home for the people who lived there.

▼ **A construction crew uses horses, picks and shovels to widen Yonge Street to accommodate new streetcar tracks in 1923.** This picture was taken looking north on Yonge, near Glengrove Avenue, just before the entrance to Lawrence Park.

Construction workers in Toronto have traditionally been Italian, although other ethnic groups have been well represented on work crews. Men who worked with stone, earth and brick all their lives on terraced farms in Italy brought their expertise to the streets of Toronto. The building boom in the twenties owed much to the backbreaking work that these men carried out. Widening and paving roads, laying streetcar tracks, building house after house in new subdivisions, digging sewers, constructing the new skyscrapers downtown — Italians were involved in all these projects.

Hiring immigrants made good business sense. An architectural firm with a building project would hire a contractor to provide and supervise the labour. A foreman, or *padrone,* had large groups of men available for work. They worked hard, the foremen kept them in line and, until they were more acclimatized, the labourers did not join unions and strike for more pay. The working conditions were often brutal, and safety was not a priority. Unfortunately, accidents and fatalities were commonplace.

136

◄ **A group of recent immigrants poses outside the British Welcome and Welfare League, April 1926.** The British Welcome and Welfare League was an organization sponsored by the British government. Its purpose was to give aid to new British immigrants to Canada, and the league helped newcomers find housing and work.

▲ **The British Welcome and Welfare League headquarters at Gerrard and Pembroke streets, 1940.**

▲ **Oakland Dairy delivers milk from a horse-drawn wagon and a truck, 1928.** Both the past and the future of transportation in Toronto are well represented in this photo. Although milk was delivered by horse into the late 1940s, the motor vehicle was taking over Toronto streets. In 1921 there were 32,000 cars and 6,200 trucks in the city. Just four years later, in 1925, the number of cars had doubled to 63,000, and there were 8,500 trucks. In 1930, there were 104,600 cars and 14,200 trucks.

▲ **Horses wait in the bitter cold as the iceman unloads a block of ice to deliver to a residence, January 1924.** The large iron grips used to lift the ice are just visible on the sleigh beside the frozen block. Throughout the twenties and into the thirties, the old-fashioned icebox was stocked with blocks that had been cut from frozen lakes or rivers. Of all the new major appliances run by electricity, the refrigerator was the last to be widely accepted by the public. In 1925 only one percent of homes in Ontario owned an electric refrigerator. By the mid-1930s, however, the public had taken to the new appliance, and the use of block ice fell off.

▼ **Ragged children, searching for lumps of coal, sort through discarded cinders dumped by the gas company, 1923.** Coal cinders were the byproduct of the process used to make coal gas — the main source of gas in Toronto until the 1950s, when natural gas began to replace it. In the twenties and thirties the widespread use of electricity and improved electric appliances offered serious competition to the gas industry.

Scrounging coal provided some extra fuel for poor families who struggled to keep their houses warm each winter. A small house required between five and seven tons of coal each winter, while big houses took as many as 50 tons to heat. A series of coal shortages during the war prompted the city to regulate prices. People sometimes lined up for hours to buy coal, and stories were told of families burning fences and furniture for fuel. Heatless days were organized. Various businesses closed down for a day at a time to save on fuel, while some families doubled up to heat just one house instead of two. Once the war ended, so did the coal shortages — until the U.S. coal miners' strikes in 1922. Since most of Toronto's fuel came from the United States, the strikes caused serious shortages in the city.

▶ **205 Ontario Street, August 1931.** This picture of two children, a bicycle and a car outside a small house was taken by Eric Arthur, the architect and preservationist who wrote *Toronto, No Mean City*. It offers us a glimpse of a sleepy street scene on a hot summer day.

◀ **Looking north from Queen and Yonge streets, April 1938.** Yonge Street bustles with life on this early spring day. Torontonians can duck into Woolworth's, buy a Holland rose bush for 25 cents, inspect Heintzman pianos across the street, or see Nelson Eddy and Jeanette MacDonald in *Girl of the Golden West* at the Loew's cinema.

The old streetcar in this picture is about to become redundant. The Toronto Transportation Commission bought 140 single-operator PCC streetcars that spring, specially developed by the President's Conference Committee of North America. The lightweight, high-performance new trams (with just a hint of Art Deco influence in their streamlined design) were operated by a single driver — an essential savings for the TTC. Annual ridership had plummeted with the sinking economy of the thirties and the popularity of the automobile. The year 1933 saw a low of 148 million passengers, down from the high of 200 million in 1929. The TTC responded to the decline by reducing its staff by 25 percent.

◄ Some things never change. In 1936, bridesmaid dresses required a certain degree of courage from the women wearing them.

▲ A newly married couple of Eastern European heritage pose for a wedding picture in a Palmerston Street living room.

◀ **The Ontario Society of Artists (OSA) Hanging Committee selects pictures at the Art Gallery of Toronto, March 1926.** Left to right: F.S. Haines, OSA president; T.W. Mitchell; Alfred Howell (sculptor); Florence Wyle (sculptor); and Arthur Lismer (member of the Group of Seven).

▼ **A man filming the Toronto skyline from a northern vantage point, late 1920s.** The tower of City Hall is visible against the outline of the Bank of Commerce Building, just right of centre, with the harbour and the Toronto Island in the background. The church spire to the left of the man's shoulder is probably that of St. James's Cathedral at King and Church streets.

By 1920 the motion picture camera had been around for nearly 30 years. The thriving U.S. film industry was churning out movies to feed the public's insatiable demand. The advent of the talkies in 1927 ushered in a new roster of movie stars and spurred the construction of palatial movie theatres. During the twenties and thirties, Toronto moviegoers could take their pick of several theatres, including Shea's Hippodrome on Bay Street, Loew's and the Tivoli on Yonge, the Uptown at Yonge and Bloor, the Hollywood at Yonge and St. Clair, the Fox in the Beaches, and the Eglinton near Avenue Road (an Art Deco gem).

Rain can't keep the punters away on opening day at Woodbine Race Track, 1928.
Overlooking the lake and just south of Queen Street and west of Woodbine Avenue, the track opened in 1874. Seven years later the Ontario Jockey Club was formed and, in 1883, Woodbine became the permanent home of the Queen's Plate (which becomes the King's Plate when the reigning monarch is male).

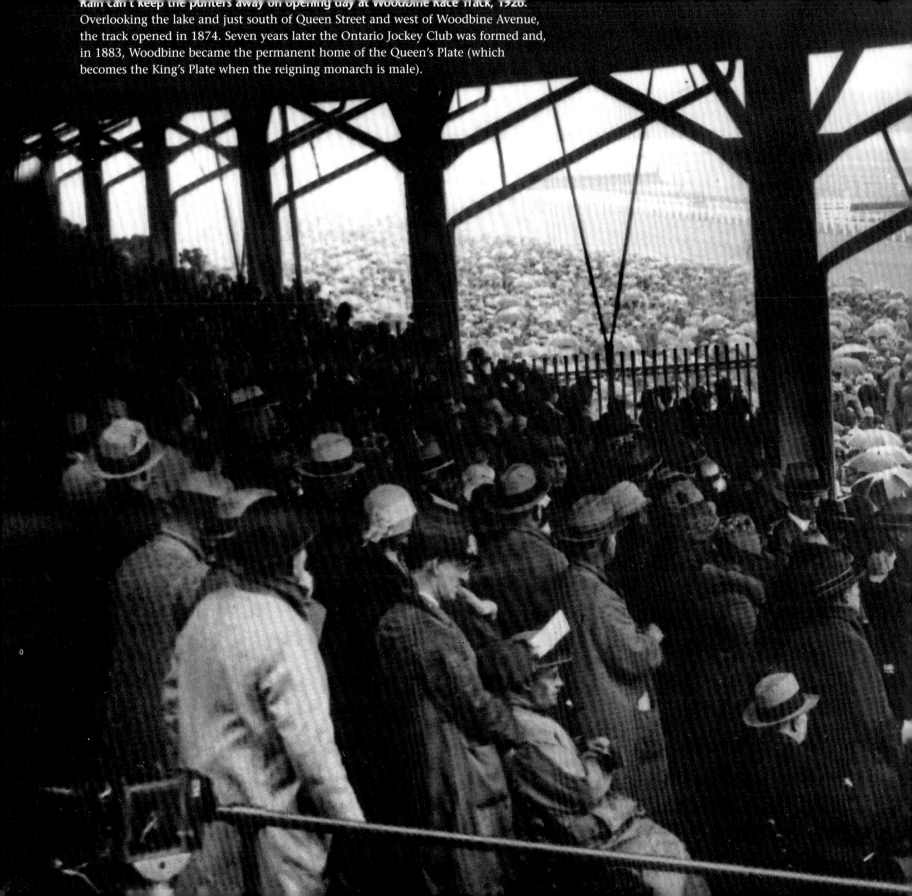

◀ **Three fashionably dressed women at Woodbine Race Track, September 1926.** Woodbine was a favourite destination for Torontonians throughout these two decades, despite a concentrated effort in the early twenties by the morally upstanding United Farmers of Ontario government to quash betting and limit the profits of the Ontario Jockey Club. New betting regulations to limit wins were enforced by the wet-blanketing presence of Mounties at all racing tracks but, despite the government's efforts, people kept having fun.

▶ **Four of Toronto's elite examine their racing cards at Woodbine Race Track, circa 1930.** Left to right: Murray P. Fleming, an avid horseman and man-about-town; Margaret Eaton; George Drew; and Mrs. R.Y. Eaton. George Drew served as Conservative premier of Ontario from 1943 to 1948. Mrs. R.Y. Eaton was married to then–department store president R.Y. Eaton, who took over when Jack Eaton died prematurely in 1922. Her children, including Margaret, had been brought up in a life of privilege. Margaret spent two years in the south of France learning French, and later was presented at Buckingham Palace. She served in the Canadian Women's Army Corps during the Second World War and rose to the position of director general.

◄ **An exciting race has the spectators enthralled at Woodbine, circa 1930.** Note the top hats. Going to the races provided an opportunity for fashionable Torontonians to put on the ritz. The highlight of the season was the annual King's Plate race in May.

▲ **King George VI and Queen Elizabeth ride in an open carriage to attend the King's Plate at Woodbine Race Track, May 1939.** This was the first time a monarch attended the King's Plate. Usually the governor general attended the race in his official capacity as the king's representative, arriving in ceremonial splendour in a four-horse barouche with postilions before and footmen behind. Queen Victoria initiated the race in 1859, when she gave a purse of 50 guineas as the prize for a race named for her.

The royal visit to Canada in 1939 was the king's first Commonwealth mission, strategically planned to rally support for the coming war. The King and Queen were greeted by eager crowds wherever they went. The Queen's evident charm and characteristic wave of the hand endeared her to the public, and great respect was given the shy and serious king, who had stepped into his brother's shoes after the abdication three years earlier. The royal couple travelled in motorcades throughout the city, greeted by cheering throngs of Torontonians eager to display their loyalty and love of pageantry. At a ceremony in Riverdale Park, where the sloping hills form a natural amphitheatre, 75,000 Toronto schoolchildren gathered on the flats while 100,000 spectators crowded on the hills to watch as the cavalry escorted the royal car into the site. The couple made a poignant stop at the Christie Street Military Hospital, where they visited veterans of the First World War. The shadow of the last war loomed large over this visit, with the certain knowledge that another war was inevitable.

▲ **Lady Eaton and Aemilius Jarvis, a Toronto financier, share a stirrup cup at the Eaton Hall Farm, King City, late 1930s.** With the stately stone mansion behind them and the very correct riding outfits, the "more British than the Brits" effect is deliberate. Lady Eaton was, after all, the widow of a knight, Sir John (Jack) Craig Eaton, and the queen of the Eaton empire. The couple had begun planning the country estate before Jack died. After living in Florence for a few years after his death, Lady Eaton returned to Canada and built Eaton Hall as her permanent home, where she and her children could indulge their passion for horseback riding. The family bred hunters, and Lady Eaton made a practice of inviting members from the Toronto and North York clubs to huntbreakfasts on her 300-acre property. The 35-room house was built to resemble a 16th-century Norman château with red tile roofs and turrets. Known to some members of her family as "Flora's Folly," Eaton Hall replaced Ardwold, the mansion Jack had built on the escarpment east of Casa Loma in 1911. Lady Eaton had Ardwold demolished in 1936 and the land divided and sold to developers.

▶ **Casa Loma, circa 1930.** At the time this photo was taken, Casa Loma had left its days of grandeur behind. When Sir Henry Pellatt faced financial ruin in the early twenties, he was forced to sacrifice his dream castle, selling off its contents at a fraction of their cost. Casa Loma enjoyed a brief reincarnation that decade as a luxury hotel and popular nightspot featuring dancing to the Casa Loma Orchestra — a swing band that went on to success in the United States after a brief stint at the hotel. But when the Royal York Hotel opened its doors in 1929, boasting lavish accommodations in a much more accessible area, it was already clear that the small, exclusive hotel could not survive. Casa Loma remained in a state of white elephantine limbo — a large, derelict reminder of better days — until the Kiwanis Club came to an arrangement with the city (which had acquired it in lieu of back taxes) and opened it as a tourist attraction in 1937.

◄ **An impressive procession at a function at the Canadian National Exhibition, early 1930s.** The dignitaries are dressed in the top hats and tails that were *de rigueur* for formal occasions at the time. The man with the beard, centre, is Sir William Mulock, chancellor of the University of Toronto and chief justice of Ontario at the time. Second from left is Conservative prime minister R.B. Bennett, who won the 1930 election by promising to fight the Depression. Once in power, his attempts to improve the economy were ineffectual, and Canadians blamed him for the desperate conditions across the country. He was defeated in the 1935 election by Liberal William Lyon Mackenzie King.

▲ **The Eaton mausoleum at Mount Pleasant Cemetery, circa 1930.** This Roman temple, built by Timothy Eaton in 1887, 20 years before he died, reflected the Eaton family's wealth and position in Toronto society. Timothy was succeeded by his son John Craig (Jack), who had been brought up in luxury with no clear idea of how ordinary people lived. Jack inherited Timothy Eaton's patriarchal attitude toward the store and its employees. He continued his father's Methodist-inspired traditions of hiding the display windows on Sundays (by closing curtains over them) and banning the sale of liquor, cigarettes and playing cards from all Eaton's stores. Jack himself had a passion for 20th-century technology, particularly cars and telephones, and owned an impressive collection of automobiles. His generous war effort during the First World War included outfitting an entire unit, called the Eaton Machine Gun Battery. This contribution earned him his knighthood.

In 1922 the dynasty took a detour with Jack's premature demise at the age of 46 after a nasty flu developed into pneumonia. His son John David was only 13, so Jack's cousin, Robert Young (R.Y.) Eaton, took charge for the next 20 years, until John David was ready to run the business.

▶ **Lady Eaton and her son John David Eaton alight from their car on their way to open the College Street Eaton's store in October 1930.** Even though R.Y. Eaton was president of the company, John David conducted the opening ritual by unlocking the door with a golden key. John David was not to become president of Eaton's until 12 years after this picture was taken, but his place at the opening ceremonies proclaimed him as prince-in-waiting. And Lady Eaton is carrying out her role to perfection: the grande dame of Toronto appearing before the adoring multitudes.

Well might she smile. She was about to witness the completion of what she thought would be the first stage of an undertaking that had been dear to her late husband's heart, as well as to her own. The new seven-storey store was intended to be the base of a 36-storey skyscraper that would house all of Eaton's offices, factories and workshops along with the elegant new store. Unfortunately, the Depression and poor planning intervened, and the rest of the project came to naught. Her particular project, the seventh floor, was not to open until the following March. Featuring Eaton's auditorium, foyer, Round Room restaurant and reception rooms designed by architect Jacques Carlu, it proved to be the crowning glory of the building.

Lady Eaton held an esteemed position in Toronto society, both before and after her husband's death. Her somewhat humble past as Flora McCrae, a student nurse from Omemee, Ontario, was all but forgotten over the years as she presided over what was unofficially Toronto's First Family. She and Sir John lived very rich, privileged lives, travelling in luxury all over the world, and considered England and Italy their second homes. She continued to cross the Atlantic after her husband's death and, during the Depression, she had houses in both France and Italy while maintaining a proprietorial interest in the business of the Eaton's empire.

One of her ocean voyages, on the *SS Île de France,* inspired the seventh-floor project. The designer of the salons in the luxury liner was Jacques Carlu, a professor of design at the Massachusetts Institute of Technology. Carlu's use of the streamlined Art Moderne style and innovative materials impressed her with its sleek elegance. She hired him to create a cultural showplace in the new Eaton's store. Her plan was to provide an elegant restaurant where ladies would lunch, some additional serving rooms, and a concert hall that could also be used for balls and banquets. Jacques Carlu surpassed all expectations in his creation of the glamorous seventh floor, hailed by many as one of the masterpieces of Art Deco in North America.

◀ **Looking south on Bay Street from the steps of Old City Hall, late 1920s.** This picture was taken when skyscrapers began to rise along Bay and the adjoining streets. The 10-storey Temple Building (centre right) with its signature turret had been a landmark since 1895, one of the first buildings in Toronto to experiment with the skyscraper concept: a building tall enough to need elevators and supported by an iron or steel skeleton. The International Order of Foresters, a men's service club, had its North American headquarters here, with club rooms and office space; hence the "IOF" on the square tower. The taller, not-yet-completed building behind it is the Sterling Tower at Richmond and Bay, which reached 20 storeys when finished in 1929.

▲ **On "Tag Day," May 1, 1924, these three young women sell tags to raise money for the blind.** Every year since the war, women raised money on Tag Day by canvassing the public on downtown streets. They also left "tag bags" in public schools (for students to fill) and collected money from commuters at the radial railway terminals. On this particular day in 1924, these women — and many others like them around the city — raised a total of $39,503.75.

▶ **A family takes the weight off their feet at the Canadian National Exhibition, August 1926.** The bags of giveaways and everyone's satisfied expression suggest that they've been having a great day at the Ex. Since Toronto became the exhibition's permanent home in 1878, the CNE has brought each summer to a close with an exuberant celebration of Canadian life: agricultural exhibitions, fairground rides, the ever-popular freak show and a string of carnies ready to take money from the unsuspecting at games of "skill and chance" on the midway. In the glory days of the Ex, new inventions were proudly displayed and governments indulged in earnest propaganda. Bicycle races, marathon swimming races, the latest car models, air shows and the entertainment at the grandstand attracted thousands of visitors each year.

◀ **A crowd mills outside the Ringling Brothers' Circus tent, 1920s.** The arrival of the circus always brought a sense of excitement and a hint of the exotic. In 1907 Ringling Brothers purchased their biggest rival, the Barnum and Bailey Circus, but the two productions continued to operate independently until about 1919, when they joined forces. The Greatest Show on Earth then became what was the largest travelling circus to date. The circus travelled from city to city across North America, packing its tents, animals and 1,200 employees into 100 double-length railway cars. The U.S. army was so impressed by the circus's organizational skills (unloading train cars, setting up tents, feeding performers and then packing everything up again) that, shortly before the First World War, it sent observers to study procedures. But, to the average Toronto citizen in this crowd, the circus provided a night of magic and fun, with elephants, clowns, acrobats and, of course, the freaks. One can't help wondering, after examining this picture, just what made William transparent.

▶ **Fairgoers leaving the Canadian National Exhibition by the Dufferin Gates, 1921.** These handsome gates were built in 1910 by architect G.W. Gouinlock, who was responsible for the grand style of the CNE buildings and grounds. He was commissioned to redesign the west end of the site. The ornate exhibit halls and the broad boulevards that defined this part of the Exhibition all bore the stamp of his vision, which was based on the 1893 World's Columbian Exposition in Chicago.

The theme of the CNE in 1921 was "National Progress," as displayed on the pillars in front of the gates. Most years the Exhibition had either a general theme to tie exhibits together or a celebration, such as the CNE's "Golden Jubilee" in 1928 and "Coronation Year" in 1937. Some other themes between the wars were "Work and Prosper" (1920), "Industry, Thrift, Prosperity" (1922), "Power, Courage, Faith" (1933), "Ties That Bind" (1925) and "Recovery Year" (1936). Most years attendance averaged about 1.5 million people, with 1,201,000 visitors in 1919 and 1,626,000 in 1939. The Golden Jubilee Year in 1928 recorded the greatest number of visitors during this time — 2,039,000 guests, many of them arriving through this ornate entrance.

◀ **Police Chief Draper leads a contingent of his Toronto policemen in the annual Warriors' Day Parade, Canadian National Exhibition, circa 1928.** The dirigible sailing by above the crowds must have added an extra thrill, for airships were a rare sight. The Electrical Building in the background, completed in 1928, served as a brightly lit demonstration of the wonders of electricity throughout the evening activities at the CNE. Constructed by the same architectural firm that built the Princes' Gates (Chapman and Oxley), it was made of poured concrete and featured a large colonnade (visible here). All exhibits were dedicated to new engineering and electrical technology. Visitors could examine and even buy the latest in electric household appliances, from irons to stoves.

PREVIOUS PAGE: **Crowds on the midway at the Canadian National Exhibition, August 1925.** Each August, a few acres of quiet parkland and ornate buildings by the lake were transformed into a noisy, thrilling, people-packed fun fair, with a wide variety of entertainment. From the seedy midway filled with opportunities to win games of chance, rides (like the famous Flyer roller coaster pictured here) and intriguing freak shows, to the Automotive Building where the latest developments in shiny cars were unveiled, to the government buildings and home-craft exhibits, to the extravagant historical pageants in the grandstand (where the most popular shows set fire to their sets just for fun), the Ex was an event you just couldn't afford to miss. In September it all closed down again as people turned their attention back to serious business. The park lay mostly deserted until the next summer.

◀ **A workman cleans the statue of Queen Victoria at Queen's Park, circa 1920.** Canadian soldiers had recently returned from fighting alongside Britain on European soil, where 60,611 Canadians had sacrificed their lives. The majority of the population had British ancestors, and most of the new immigrants to Toronto came from Britain. "God Save the King" was the Canadian national anthem, and the Union Jack was part of the national flag. The devastation of the war had shaken some of the country's faith in Britain, and U.S. influence was crossing the border in the form of radio, movies, newspapers and magazines. Yet loyalty to Britain and reverence for the royal family and what they stood for remained strong.

▶ **The parking lot at Maple Leaf Stadium, Bathurst Street and Lakeshore Boulevard, 1932.** The 20,000-seat stadium, which opened in 1926, was home to the Toronto Maple Leafs baseball team from 1926 to 1967. The team's owner, "Lol" Solman, built the stadium as the result of an on-going battle with the city. Previously the Maple Leafs had played at Hanlan's Point on the Toronto Island. Solman owned the ferries that transported fans to the game, but when the city expropriated his company he built a new stadium on the Toronto side of the channel — just to spite the new owner. Fans no longer took the ferries to the games, and the city lost revenue. The new stadium was lucky for the Toronto baseball team: that first season the players won the Little World Series championship, and they later won five more pennants and four Governor's Cup championships at this location. The Tip Top Tailors Building is visible in the upper-right corner of the photo, and the Princes' Gates and CNE buildings lie beyond.

◄ One of the judges of the baby contest holds the first-prize winner, Canadian National Exhibition, 1925.

► **Baby and her mother at the CNE Baby Show, 1926.** Contestants in the Baby Show came from all over Ontario and the northern United States to compete in eight classes divided by age and gender, with special categories for twins. The grand champion was chosen from the winners of each class. The criteria for a prize-winning baby included health, cleanliness, neatness and general appearance, and prizes consisted of cash and souvenir CNE medallions. Families were warned on the entry forms that "judges will not enter into a discussion with parents regarding babies," and that "all decisions ... are final." These regulations hint of occasional rancour among parents whose babies were not awarded prizes. But each of these contenders displays the qualities of a prize-winning baby, circa 1920s: plump, clean, a modest amount of neatly kept hair and a thoughtful expression.

▲ **Boys line up for the schoolboys' bicycle race at the CNE grandstand, circa 1926.** The grandstand, like the larger CNE experience, offered a range of events for participants and spectators. Bicycle racing had been part of the Ex since 1880. It grew to be a popular annual event, with open, handicap and invitational races covering one-, three- and five-mile courses.

► **Looking north on Bay Street to City Hall, Christmas Eve, 1924.** It looks like a very cold Christmas Eve. Horses were still a common sight in the centre of the city, as were policemen directing traffic. Signal lights would not be introduced for another three years.

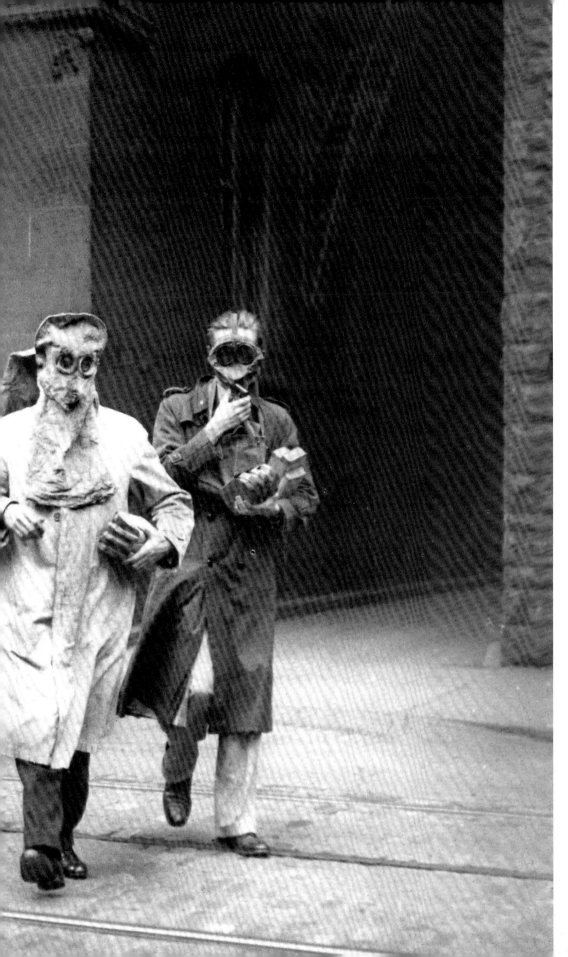

◀ **League of Nations Society protesters in gas masks cross Adelaide Street, April 17, 1936.** Germany had invaded the Rhineland in March 1936, just a month before this picture was taken in downtown Toronto. Under the heading "Grim Reminder of What Next War May Bring," the caption with this picture described the demonstration: about a dozen men in gas masks appeared on the streets at lunch time, distributing bomb-shaped pamphlets that outlined the costs of the last war in terms of lives and money.

In 1921 the League of Nations Society was formed in Canada by citizens who supported the newly fledged league. The international organization had come into being in 1920, in the wake of the peace settlement of the First World War. Its goal was to avoid further armed conflicts by working toward the peaceful settlement of disputes between member countries. The league also promoted humanitarian aid and decreased weaponry. It used economic sanctions against member countries that went to war and refused to abide by its arbitration system. Initially 41 nations joined the organization, later augmented by 20 more.

Throughout the twenties the League of Nations operated with some success but, by the 1930s, the rising support for Hitler and Mussolini and various disputes and withdrawals of member countries contributed to the weakening and ultimate failure of the league. Its successor was the United Nations, established after the Second World War.

In Canada the League of Nations Society promoted the goals of the League of Nations by working to educate Canadians about international affairs, the first Canadian organization to do so. Several prominent Canadian figures were involved in the society, including Sir Robert Borden, who had been Canada's prime minister during the First World War, and Co-operative Commonwealth Federation (CCF) founder J.S. Woodsworth. The society distributed literature and sponsored speaking tours and radio broadcasts to promote interest and support for the League of Nations.

◄ **Looking south from St. Clair Avenue and Avenue Road, 1939.** By 1939 the automobile dominated Toronto streets. This looks like the evening rush hour, with heavy traffic going north and the Peter Witt streetcars turning west onto St. Clair. The Toronto Transportation Commission bought 575 steel Peter Witt streetcars in 1921, their first year of operation, and in 1938 it purchased 140 President's Conference Committee (PCC) streetcars. The PCC's big advantage was that it could be operated by only one person, thus cutting down on costs.

▶ **The aftermath of an ugly accident between an old streetcar and a truck on Danforth Avenue, probably in the early 1920s.** Between 1916 and 1928 the number of automobiles in Toronto rose from 10,000 to 80,000. In the same space of time, the number of commercial vehicles jumped from 1,000 to 13,000. Even though the speed limit was a sluggish 15 miles per hour, the streets were filled with vehicles — and some nasty encounters occurred. In 1924, 55 people died from injuries sustained in car accidents. With uneven road surfaces in various states of repair, no traffic lights and minimal safety rules, driving in Toronto was even more of a risk than it is today. It looks as though this streetcar burned after the impact. Note the gas pump at the side of the road, with no setback for safety or place for passengers to stop that wouldn't block traffic.

◄ A newspaper stand at King and Yonge streets, September 1925.

▶ A Mack "shock-insulated" bus loads passengers for a demonstration run from Toronto to Montreal, June 3, 1925. As the automotive engine began to be used by all sorts of vehicles — buses, trucks, hearses, street-cleaning vehicles and more — great efforts were made to improve passenger comfort. The makers of Mack trucks, based in Allentown, Pennsylvania, produced this shock-insulated bus in the mid-1920s. It featured a less bumpy ride, thanks to the use of rubber mounts and bushings. A demonstration trip took a select group of passengers from Toronto to Montreal on this late spring day, although regular service between the cities was not introduced until 1935, when Colonial Coach Lines scheduled a regular run.

In 1927 the Toronto Transportation Commission branched out by incorporating the Gray Coach Lines bus system, which provided transportation to North Bay, London, Buffalo and other cities. Gray Coach introduced a bus with technological innovations that included a hot-water heating system for those cold runs in December, engines in the back (to reduce noise and vibration), four-wheel brakes and weatherproof baggage compartments underneath the bus — much preferable to the exposed roof racks used previously. The bus business was so successful that in 1931 the TTC built the Art Deco bus terminal at Bay and Edward streets that still stands today. After 1934, a favourite stop on the North Bay bus run was Callander, Ontario, where the Dionne quintuplets were on public display.

183

◄ **Spadina Avenue, north of King Street, 1928.** When William Baldwin laid out Spadina Avenue in 1836, he created one of the broadest streets in Toronto, at 132 feet wide. He also planted imported chestnut trees, creating the boulevard. These trees and their descendants were removed to create more room for traffic in 1928 (about a month after this picture was taken). In the twenties the city initiated an extensive street improvement program to accommodate the growing number of cars. By the end of the decade there were more than a hundred thousand cars in Toronto. Streets were widened and extended, and some major intersections were realigned. Carlton and College streets did not meet at Yonge until 1929, when Carlton was widened to eliminate the 689-foot jog westbound that streetcars had to take up Yonge Street. Bridges were upgraded and underpasses were built to eliminate long waits at level crossings.

▶ **Contestants in a skijoring race line up in High Park, waiting for the word "Go," February 1926.** Skijoring is something like waterskiing on snow, with the skier behind a horse instead of a boat.

Outdoor recreation in Toronto took many forms throughout the seasons. In winter High Park provided hills for skiing and tobogganing, frozen Grenadier Pond for skating, rinks for hockey, trails for walking, and open spaces for the intrepid skijorers. In spring, summer and autumn, the Humber River enticed fishermen, boaters and swimmers. For those who liked to belong to clubs, Toronto offered a variety of amusements: quoits, lawn bowling, canoeing, sailing, cricket and riding. By 1929 the city boasted 38 neighbourhood parks, and in 1931 it spent about $19 million on recreation and education — roughly double the 1920 expenditure. As Toronto developed as a modern industrial centre, it began maturing into a city whose residents could live well and enjoy the outdoors. The tally of public park facilities in 1929: 1,662 acres of parks, 83 baseball diamonds, 5 lacrosse fields, 261 tennis courts, 62 skating rinks and 60 hockey rinks.

▶ **Boys fishing on the Humber River for perch and catfish, circa 1924.**

◄ **Boys playing a fierce game of hockey in High Park, 1925.** The caption with this picture (taken by *Globe* photographer John Boyd) read: "The secret of Canada's success in hockey is that the players begin young. These lads are hard at the game in the new rink opened by the city on Parkside Drive."

◄ **Members of the Queen City Quoit Club at Trinity College, 1923.** Quoits is a game similar to horseshoes.

▲ **Looking down on Bloor Street and a crowd at Varsity Stadium, 1930s.**
The building just right of centre was occupied by the Meteorological Service
of Canada, which until 1971 provided weather forecasts and storm warnings.

A number of the buildings that defined Bloor between St. George Street
and Avenue Road in the twenties and thirties are still there: the Medical Arts
Building (1929), the York Club (1892; formerly George Gooderham's house),
the Meteorological Building (1909), the Royal Conservatory of Music (1881),
the Royal Ontario Museum (1914), the Park Plaza Hotel (1929; now the Park
Hyatt), the Church of the Redeemer (1879) and the Lillian Massey Department of Household Science (1912; now Club Monaco).

▲ **Maple Leaf Gardens packed with spectators at a hockey game, circa 1932.** This large, boxlike structure at Church and Carlton streets became part of a legend almost before it was completed. Constructed in a record five months and 12 days by a workforce driven night and day by the ambition and zeal of the Maple Leafs' owner, Conn Smythe, the arena was hailed as the best in the world. After being fired by the New York Rangers for "impudence," Smythe raised $160,000 (partly through gambling his savings, according to rumour) to buy the St. Patrick's hockey team. He renamed it the Toronto Maple Leafs and built his team a sports cathedral in which to play the game. The players repaid him by winning the Stanley Cup in 1932, in their first season in Maple Leaf Gardens. The Canadian passion for hockey was entrenched in this building during the thirties, with Foster Hewitt relaying the excitement of the games over the radio to a breathless nation. The Gardens also played host to wrestling, boxing, lacrosse, badminton, tennis and a very popular annual social event, the Toronto Skating Club Carnival, which featured the championship skaters of the day. Political rallies and religious gatherings took advantage of the spacious Gardens, as did the ballet and the opera.

▲ Policemen hold back the crowds of young fans who showed up at Sunnyside Station to witness the arrival of marathon swimming champion George Young, February 1927.

◄ Long-distance swimmer George Young waves to thousands of fans at a special reception to welcome him home outside City Hall, February 1927. A few weeks earlier, he had won the Catalina Marathon Race from Catalina Island to the California mainland. He was the only contestant to finish the gruelling 20-mile course, with a time of 15 hours, 44 minutes and 30 seconds. The prize was $25,000 and instant, enormous fame.

Long-distance swimming was wildly popular in the twenties and thirties. The Catalina race, sponsored by the chewing-gum magnate William Wrigley, was alluring because of its big cash prize. Young, a 17-year-old swimmer who grew up in Cabbage-town, began the trek from Toronto to California on an old motorcycle that got him as far as Denver, Colorado, where he hitched a ride the rest of the way. After the race he spent a few weeks in the United States, making appearances and performing a small part in a movie, before returning to Toronto. His reception was overwhelming. One hundred and fifty thousand people lined Queen Street from Sunnyside Station to City Hall, cheering him.

The CNE used his superstar status and name to initiate its own Wrigley Marathon Swim the following August. The annual event pushed up attendance records and lured contestants with fat cash prizes. The swimmers cheerfully greased themselves with a mixture of lanolin and Vaseline to keep out the cold — and then plunged into the icy waters of Lake Ontario. The course covered 21 miles. All bets were on Young to win the first one in 1927, but he developed a cramp after five miles and had to drop out. Of all the other marathon swims held at the CNE over the next few years, Young won only one, in 1931. He was then forgotten by the fickle public, although he later appeared in a swimming tank at a CNE sideshow.

▲ **A science class at Riverdale Technical School, March 11, 1926.** In the late 1920s Toronto had three technical high schools: Central Tech, Riverdale Tech and Western Tech. All high schools offered evening as well as daytime classes. In 1930, 17,000 students registered for technical night classes, about double the number of day students.

◄ **The last day of school, June 25, 1925.**

▲ **Students at High Park Forest School, May 4, 1926.** The value of fresh air as an all-purpose tonic was hailed at this time. Various experiments included a campaign to prevent tuberculosis by keeping school windows wide open all year, with the students wrapped up in coats in the winter. This dubious practice was stopped because, not surprisingly, it had a bad effect on children's health.

The forest schools' program, established in 1912, lasted longer with much better results. The two forest schools, set up for children with health, mental and behavioural problems, offered open-air study, wholesome meals and afternoon naps. One school was in High Park and the other in Victoria Park.

The students attended from May until October. The forest schools were created for children who "bear the earmarks of incipient disease and whose poverty precludes any hope of summer vacation away from the dirt and degradation of their homes." The health officials and educators responsible for the schools believed that attendance at forest schools would improve children's health, raise their energy levels and expand their capacity to learn. The program involved feeding the youngsters healthful food, giving them rest periods each day, instructing them about basic hygiene and teaching them the fundamentals of writing and arithmetic, all in the fresh open air. At the beginning of

the experiment, 70 percent of the students were immigrants. The schools emphasized assimilation and the virtues of the British Empire. But in the twenties immigration levels fell, and the mental and physical health of the children became the educators' chief concern. The idea was that the children could be returned to the regular school system after their stint in the woods. One of the easier ways to measure success was by weight, which the students at the forest schools gained steadily.

▶ **Four of the competitors in the Normal School Oratory Competition, April 3, 1936.**

▲ Girls play skipping at Annette Street Public School, March 25, 1936.

▲ Student with her cake, Central Technical School, March 4, 1936.

▶ Cooking class, Central Technical School, July 10, 1923.

▲ Children work on crafts in a Toronto auxiliary class, 1930.

▲ **A teacher administers a "mental test" to an auxiliary class student, 1930.** The late teens and early twenties saw a shift as schools provided for students who had disabilities, whether physical or mental. The Toronto Department of Health, through its regular school medical check-ups, helped to identify children with difficulties. The students were then referred to counsellors, and parents received advice about how to improve their children's chances in life. Special classes were developed for the deaf, the sight-impaired and slow learners, and the open-air forest schools continued to accommodate children with behavioural problems and poor overall health.

In 1917 a psychiatric consultant at the Toronto Department of Health, Clarence Hincks, began administering the Binet-Simon intelligence test. Children who needed help were placed in auxiliary classes. By the end of 1921 this special effort to reach slower learners was in full swing, with 21 auxiliary and industrial classes. The auxiliary classes were limited to 16 students, in contrast with the regular class complement of 45. The rationale was that by separating the children, each group would get more of the teacher's attention, and the students in the auxiliary classes wouldn't feel worried about lagging behind their peers.

▼ **Students at Northern Vocational School demonstrate their skills, March 1936.** These high school students, training for jobs in the commercial sector, use the office equipment of the day: the dictaphone with earphones, the telephone switchboard and the typewriter.

▼ **A student operates heavy machinery at a technical school, March 12, 1936.** In the early 1920s, municipal politicians, newspapers and the public were involved in a long and heated debate over additional education spending. The outspoken mayor, Tommy Church, was agin' it, and the majority of the citizens agreed that too much was spent on "fads and frills." Although public schools were badly crowded and underfunded, Church vehemently opposed giving schools any more money and wanted to cut manual training and domestic sciences. The controversy raged on for a number of years, but spending on education gradually increased over the decade — with the average cost per student rising from $63 in 1919 to $89 in 1929 for elementary school, and from $133 to $160 for high school. In the Depression the technical programs were especially popular with students hoping to gain some small advantage in the job market by acquiring practical skills.

▶ **Girls participate in the Toronto Milk Campaign by drinking milk at school, 1921.** A long and hard-fought battle to deliver pure milk to Torontonians culminated in Milk Week, April 4–9, 1921. Toronto had gained an international reputation for its healthful milk, and the Toronto Health Department was considered a pioneer in the field of clean milk. In the twenties and thirties milk-borne diseases were greatly reduced throughout the city, and citizens could drink milk with confidence.

In the 1880s the Health Department found that milk sold in Toronto was "contaminated with dirt and tuberculosis bacilli, and adulterated with water, boracic [boric] or salicylic acid, and annatto [a yellowish-red dye]." Diseases transmitted through milk included tuberculosis, diphtheria, scarlet fever and typhoid. In an effort to eliminate these diseases, in the late 19th century dairy owners were required to obtain a cleanliness certificate, issued by Health Department inspectors, verifying that their premises were sanitary.

By 1911 the Ontario government had passed the *Milk Act,* which required veterinary inspectors to make thrice-yearly visits to any farm that supplied milk to the city's dairies. They were to check cows and buildings and examine workers for signs of typhoid or tuberculosis. In the city, dairies and stores selling milk were inspected for sanitation. The milk itself underwent a number of tests, including one for bacteria and another for dirt, the latter performed by filtering the milk through a cotton disk. Contaminated milk was either dumped down the sewer or, in some cases, dyed red and returned to the farmer with a big red label proclaiming to his neighbours that he had sold rotten milk.

Charles Hastings was the man behind pasteurization, the Toronto Milk Campaign and Milk Week. The medical officer of health for Toronto between 1910 and 1929, Hastings had a personal interest in the delivery of pure milk, a motivation that drove him to make Toronto's milk among the safest in North America. One of his daughters had died as a baby after contracting typhoid from contaminated milk purchased from a reputable dairy. Hastings was determined to spare other parents the terrible grief of losing a child in this manner, so he made it his goal to clean up the milk in the city. The first thing he did was to trace the typhoid that had killed his daughter. His inspectors discovered that the dairy where the contaminated milk had been purchased used a contaminated well, and that one of its suppliers had typhoid. The milk crusaders' slogan, "You don't catch typhoid — you eat it or drink it," was, sadly, true in this case.

The next step for Hastings was to start an educational campaign among suppliers that would promote new technology for producing cleaner milk. Then he initiated a monthly publication called the *Health Bulletin,* which told Torontonians what the Health Department was doing for them and informed readers about international research in public health. Here he published a list of "first class dairies" — those approved by the Health Department — where consumers could be assured of buying good milk. The bulletin also promoted healthy competition among dairy owners.

Hastings also used the *Health Bulletin* to promote pasteurization, a goal that was finally realized in 1914 and which he regarded as the ultimate solution to the milk-contamination problem. The process successfully killed all the bacteria in milk, eliminating a huge cause of disease.

Unfortunately, he had an uphill battle persuading the public that pasteurization was a healthy alternative to raw milk. People believed that the procedure would kill the nutritional value of the milk and affect the flavour.

Publicity was the answer, and Hastings waded cheerfully into a very 20th-century occupation: selling his message. Using the latest advertising techniques imported from the United States, he mounted his campaign of information. He was so successful in his efforts that Toronto City Council made pasteurization of milk compulsory in 1914.

The promotion of healthful milk continued. In 1921 Hastings joined forces with the Child Welfare Council of Toronto, the Canadian Public Health Association and the National Dairy Council of Canada to sponsor Milk Week in Toronto, April 4–9. Everyone joined in the spirit of drinking milk for health, with advertising everywhere: in schools, restaurants, hotels, streetcars and specially designed department store windows. Schoolchildren wore blue buttons that proclaimed "I Drink Milk" and were given desk blotters imprinted with a cartoon "Mr. Milk Bottle" that told them "Milk Makes Muscle." They drew posters and composed jingles singing the praises of milk. At work, adults were presented with brief lectures and pamphlets covering the value of drinking milk. There was even a play about milk, performed at Massey Hall.

Charles Hastings had achieved his goal of making Toronto milk safe to drink, and the Health Department boasted that "Toronto was able to control milk production from cow to consumer." In 1938 the Ontario government finally joined the bandwagon and made pasteurization compulsory throughout the province.

205

◀ As part of the publicity for the Toronto Milk Campaign, the national health convenor, Dr. Margaret Patterson, milks a cow in a Toronto park, 1921.

◀ Workers tend a milk-bottling machine at a dairy, circa 1920.

▶ Following his daily rounds, this cheerful milkman is returning milk bottles to the dairy, circa 1920.

◀ **A fish seller displays his wares, July 1929.** Horses were used to transport anyone and anything around the city. The animals were even colour coordinated to match the corporate styles of the fashionable department stores. Eaton's traditionally used chestnut-coloured horses to pull its delivery wagons, while the slightly more upscale Simpsons preferred dapple-grey.

▶ **A thirsty horse is helped to a drink by children on a Toronto street, July 13, 1925.** Today the only horses on Toronto streets are those ridden by occasionally glimpsed mounted policemen. But in Toronto in 1920 horses were a common sight, not yet completely replaced by the omnipresent automobile. By the end of the thirties, horses could still be found pulling delivery wagons and street-cleaning carts. In 1946, however, grocery delivery by horse had tapered off and the street-cleaning department sold its last 25 horses.

Like cars, horses required a certain amount of maintenance, housing and care. One of the Street Cleaning Department's jobs was to clean up the multitude of "road apples" deposited by the horses as they carried people and goods around the city. In 1928 the department owned 400 horses, with 200 privately owned horses on call for busier times. It took considerable expense to keep so many animals, with the feed bill topping the list: hay, bran, oats, carrots and salt were necessary to keep the horses healthy. Six blacksmiths worked full-time for the department, reshoeing the horses at least once a month, and a full-time vet was on hand to attend to their ailments.

▼ **Now that the snow has melted, these two devoted mummies bring their babies out for a spring stroll, March 10, 1936.** Dolls were a favourite toy for little girls in Toronto, and the lucky ones had the fancy accoutrements like these rattan strollers. Eaton's 1926 catalogue provided a doll owner's every need. Washing sets, including tub, washboard and folding clothes dryer (with pins), could be had for $1.69; and a separate iron cost only 29 cents. A doll's bed with side-curtains and a decorated mattress was $2.25, and a little stove with removable lids and saucepans cost only 69 cents. And of course there were doll tea-sets and furniture, and even a doll-sized piano.

There was a time when no self-respecting little girl didn't own a Shirley Temple doll. But long before Shirley's arrival, Eaton's featured an annual doll called the Eaton Beauty Doll, at prices ranging from $1.50 for the 21-inch version to $5.00 for the deluxe 27-inch doll. Extra clothes could be bought separately. A set of panties, underskirt, bonnet and dress cost $1.50. Baby dolls really cried and then went to sleep, flapper dolls featured a flapper dress and cloche hat, and a June-bride doll wore appropriate attire for her wedding.

The catalogue description for the Eaton Beauty Doll in 1926 is pretty well irresistible: "She is the pride of Toyland. She stands 21 inches high, has beautiful bisque head, curly wig, lovely eyes that open and close, with long eyelashes, well formed composition body, jointed at neck, shoulders, elbows, wrists, hips and knees; wears a white slip and has dainty shoes and socks."

▲ **This picture of 15 children representing more than a dozen nationalities appeared in the *Globe* in June 1923, with the caption "In the Canadian Melting Pot."** Ethnic backgrounds were listed as follows: Front row (left to right): Danish, Bulgarian, Canadian, Chinese, Jewish, Polish, Italian, Austrian, Syrian. Back row: English, Scottish, Negro, Swiss. The children all attended York Street School.

The Union Jack draped symbolically behind these multicultural tots united them as children of the Empire. The first decades of the 20th century were marked by a fierce determination by government, educators and British-Canadian society at large to "Canadianize" the immigrants who came to settle in Canada.

The big wave of immigrants who were not British began in the late 1890s, when Clifford Sifton, the minister of the interior, began his campaign to fill Canada with people. The government and leaders of society, who were "no more racist in their thinking than the culture of their times," believed in a hierarchy of "desirable" immigrants, very much based on skin colour. First on the list were the British, of course, and white Americans. Next came Scandinavians, Germans and Ukrainians. At the lower end of the list were those with darker skin: Jews, Italians, South Slavs, Greeks, Syrians, Chinese and blacks. In the 1920s the *Chinese Immigration Act* stopped all immigration from China, and black immigrants were unofficially discouraged.

It seemed very important to many Canadians that the new citizens be schooled in British values, habits and behaviour. It was desirable that they leave their "nasty foreign ways" behind and become cardboard-cutout Canadians, washing their hands several times a day, cleaning their fingernails, eating porridge and singing "God Save the King." The schools were the place to catch them when young, and educators made an effort to instruct their charges to be more "Canadian."

▲ **Girls race at the Shriners picnic for orphans at the Toronto Island, July 1922.** Founded in the United States in 1870 as a society for Masons who had attained a certain status, the Shriners are known for their charitable work as well as their funny hats (the scarlet fez). The Toronto Shriners (Rameses Temple) was established in 1888. In 1930 Toronto played host to a huge gathering of Shriners at the 56th annual session of their imperial council. Approximately 7,000 members flooded the city and entertained themselves and the citizens of Toronto by marching in parades. Between 100,000 and 120,000 people turned out to see the fun, which included 65 massed bands and 2,275 marchers. The strain on hotels was so great that the overflow of Shriners had to be accommodated on a ship in

the harbour and in a temporary city in the railway yards near
Fort York. "Fez City" provided each of its inhabitants with a bed
in one of the 350 sleeping cars set out on 12 miles of tracks, with
heat and ventilation supplied by three locomotives. It also offered
a restaurant, newsstand, showers, barber shop, information bureau
and taxi stand.

▲ Men pressing Canadian army uniforms in a Toronto
clothing factory, in preparation for war, December 1939.

References

The 1996 Canadian Encyclopedia Plus. Toronto: McClelland and Stewart, 1995, on CD-ROM.

Armstrong, Frederick H. *Toronto: The Place of Meeting, An Illustrated History.* Toronto: Windsor Publications in cooperation with the Ontario Historical Society, 1983.

Bébout, Richard, editor (with commentary on historical photographs by Mike Filey). *The Open Gate: Toronto Union Station.* Toronto: Peter Martin Associates, 1972.

Berton, Pierre. *The Great Depression: 1929–1939.* Toronto: McClelland and Stewart, 1990.

Blum, Stella. *Everyday Fashions of the Thirties.* New York: Dover Publications, 1986.

Broadfoot, Barry. *Ten Lost Years: 1929–1939.* Toronto: McClelland and Stewart, 1973.

Brown, Craig, editor. *The Illustrated History of Canada.* Toronto: Lester and Orpen Dennys, 1987.

Brown, Ron. *Toronto's Lost Villages.* Toronto: Polar Bear Press, 1997.

Burrill, William. *Hemingway: The Toronto Years 1920–24.* Toronto: Doubleday, 1994.

Compton's Encyclopedia. Novato, Calif.: The Learning Company, 1999, on CD-ROM.

Crawford, Bess Hillery. *Rosedale.* Erin, Ontario: Boston Mills Press, 2000.

Creighton, Donald. *Canada's First Century: 1867–1967.* Toronto: Macmillan, 1970.

———. *The Story of Canada.* Toronto: Macmillan, 1959.

Dendy, William. *Lost Toronto* (second edition). Toronto: McClelland and Stewart, 1993.

Dendy, William, and William Kilbourn. *Toronto Observed: Its Architecture, Patrons and History.* Toronto: Oxford University Press, 1986.

Donegan, Rosemary. *Spadina Avenue.* Toronto: Douglas and McIntyre, 1985.

Eaton's Spring and Summer Catalogue, 1927. Toronto: Musson Book Company, 1971.

Eaton's Spring and Summer Catalogue, 1936. Toronto: T. Eaton Company, 1936.

Ege, Lennart. *Balloons and Airships, 1793–1973.* London: Blandford Press, 1973.

Filey, Mike. *A Toronto Album: Glimpses of the City That Was.* Toronto: Dundurn Press, 2001.

———. *Toronto Sketches: "The Way We Were."* Toronto: Dundurn Press, 1992.

Filey, Mike, and Victor Russell. *From Horse Power to Horsepower: Toronto 1890–1930.* Toronto: Dundurn Press, 1993.

Gatenby, Greg. *Toronto: A Literary Guide.* Toronto: McArthur and Company, 1999.

Glazebrook, G.P. de T. *The Story of Toronto.* Toronto: University of Toronto Press, 1971.

Glazebrook, G.P. de T., Katherine B. Brett and Judith McErvel. *A Shopper's View of Canada's Past.* Toronto: University of Toronto Press, 1969.

Guillet, Edwin C. *Toronto: Trading Post to Great City.* Toronto: Ontario Publishing Company, 1934.

Harney, Robert F. *Gathering Place: Peoples and Neighbourhoods of Toronto, 1834–1945.* Toronto: Multicultural History Society of Ontario, 1985.

Harney, Robert, and Harold Troper. *Immigrants: A Portrait of the Urban Experience, 1890–1930.* Toronto: Van Nostrand Reinhold, 1975.

Hume, Christopher. *William James's Toronto Views: Lantern Slides from 1906 to 1939.* Toronto: James Lorimer and Company, 1999.

Jones, Donald. *Fifty Tales of Toronto.* Toronto: University of Toronto Press, 1992.

Kilbourn, William. *The Making of the Nation: A Century of Challenge.* Toronto: Canadian Centennial Publishing Company, 1965.

Kluckner, Michael. *Toronto: The Way It Was.* Toronto: Whitecap Books, 1988.

Lemon, James. *Toronto Since 1918: An Illustrated History.* Toronto: James Lorimer and Company and National Museum of Man, 1985.

Lundell, Liz. *The Estates of Old Toronto.* Erin, Ontario: Boston Mills Press, 1997.

MacDougall, Heather. *Activists and Advocates: Toronto's Health Department, 1883–1983.* Toronto: Dundurn Press, 1990.

Martyn, Lucy Booth. *Aristocratic Toronto: 19th Century Grandeur.* Toronto: Gage Publishing, 1980.

McHugh, Patricia. *Toronto Architecture: A City Guide* (second edition). Toronto: McClelland and Stewart, 1989.

McQueen, Rod. *The Eatons: The Rise and Fall of Canada's Royal Family.* Toronto: Stoddart, 1998.

Ritchie, Don. *North Toronto.* Toronto: Stoddart, 1992.

Stamp, Robert M. *Bright Lights, Big City: The History of Electricity in Toronto.* Toronto: Ontario Association of Archivists, Toronto Chapter, 1991.

Stephenson, William. *The Store That Timothy Built.* Toronto: McClelland and Stewart, 1969.

West, Bruce. *Toronto.* Toronto: Doubleday, 1967.

White, Randall. *Toronto Women: Changing Faces 1900–2000, A Photographic Journey.* Toronto: Eastend Books, 1997.

———. *Too Good To Be True: Toronto in the 1920s.* Toronto: Dundurn Press, 1993.

———. *Ontario 1610–1985: A Political and Economic History.* Toronto: Dundurn Press, 1985.

Wise, Leonard, and Allan Gould. *Toronto Street Names: An Illustrated Guide to Their Origins.* Toronto: Firefly Books, 2000.

Photo Credits

Cover: City of Toronto Archives, Series 71, Item 12453   **2** Archives of Ontario, C 7-3, 18635   **5** City of Toronto Archives, Fonds 1244, Item 978   **7** City of Toronto Archives, Globe and Mail Collection, Fonds 1266, Item 6710   **8** Private Collection   **11** City of Toronto Archives, Globe and Mail Collection, Fonds 1266, Item 5712   **12** Metro Toronto Reference Library, 974-11-4   **16/17** City of Toronto Archives, Globe and Mail Collection, Fonds 1266, Item 8495   **18** City of Toronto Archives, Fonds 1244, Item 8198   **19** City of Toronto Archives, Globe and Mail Collection,   Fonds 1266, Item 7330   **20/21** City of Toronto Archives, Fonds 1231, Item 2089   **22/23** Toronto Star File Photo, Product Code 2559/h3rgvbz3   **24** City of Toronto Archives, Globe and Mail Collection, Fonds 1266, Item 6031   **25** City of Toronto Archives, Globe and Mail Collection, Fonds 1266, Item 7576   **26** City of Toronto Archives, Fonds 1244, Item 2394   **27** Archives of Ontario, RG 9-7-5-0-37   **28** Archives of Ontario, F229-308-0-517-7, AO 1861, Courtesy of Sears Canada Inc.   **29** Archives of Ontario, F229-308-0-520-2, AO 6238, Courtesy of Sears Canada Inc.   **30** Archives of Ontario, F229-308-1983, Courtesy of Sears Canada Inc.   **31** Archives of Ontario, F229-308-0-2325-1, AO 297, Courtesy of Sears Canada Inc.   **32** Toronto Public Library, Acc: E 1-32b, Repro: T 11076, Slide MTL 1656   **33** Archives of Ontario, RG 9-7-5-0-5   **34** Toronto Public Library, Acc: X 64-331, Repro: T 33049   **35** Archives of Ontario, RG 9-7-5-0-65   **36** City of Toronto Archives, Fonds 1244, Item 1155   **37** City of Toronto Archives, Series 71, Item 9409   **38** City of Toronto Archives, Fonds 1231, Item 478   **39** City of Toronto Archives, SC 266, Item 6724   **40** City of Toronto Archives, Globe and Mail Collection, Fonds 1266, Item 38862   **41** City of Toronto Archives, Globe and Mail Collection, Fonds 1266, Item 39564   **42/43** City of Toronto Archives, Fonds 1266, Item 1128   **44** City of Toronto Archives, Fonds 1244, Item 2466   **45** City of

Toronto Archives, Fonds 1244, Item 1798   **46/47** City of Toronto Archives, Fonds 1244, Item 1742   **48** City of Toronto Archives, Fonds 1244, Item 8050   **49** City of Toronto Archives, Fonds 1244, Item 2054   **50/51** National Archives, Acc: 1971-120, Item 18373, Repro: PA 086228   **52** City of Toronto Archives, Fonds 1244, Item 343A   **53** City of Toronto Archives, Fonds 1244, Item 8054   **54** City of Toronto Archives, Globe and Mail Collection, Fonds 1266, Item 8837   **55** City of Toronto Archives, Globe and Mail Collection, Fonds 1266, Item 8836   **56/57** City of Toronto Archives, Fonds 1244, Item 1014   **58** City of Toronto Archives, Fonds 1244, Item 1947   **59** City of Toronto Archives, Globe and Mail Collection, Fonds 1266, Item 39501   **60** City of Toronto Archives, Fonds, 1266, Item 8578   **61** City of Toronto Archives, Globe and Mail Collection, Fonds 1266, Item 5264   **62** Archives of Ontario, S 56   **63** City of Toronto Archives, Globe and Mail Collection, Fonds 1266, Item 1486   **64** City of Toronto Archives, Fonds 1244, Item 1717   **65** City of Toronto Archives, Fonds 1244, Item 1902   **66/67** City of Toronto Archives, Series 71, Item 7175   **68/69** City of Toronto Archives, Fonds 1244, Item 214   **70** City of Toronto Archives, Fonds 1244, Item 8201   **71** (upper) City of Toronto Archives, Fonds 1244, Item 1149   **71** (lower) City of Toronto Archives, Fonds 1244, Item 1151A   **72/73** City of Toronto Archives, Fonds 1244, Item 533   **74** Toronto Public Library, Acc: 980-9-587, Repro: T 30118   **75** Toronto Public Library, Acc: 942-1-61, Repro: T 10032, Slide MTL 2396   **76** Toronto Public Library, Acc: X 65-177, Repro: T 32425   **77** City of Toronto Archives, Globe and Mail Collection, Fonds 1266, Item 4966   **78** City of Toronto Archives, Fonds 1244, Item 2017   **79** City of Toronto Archives, Fonds 1244, Item 2402   **80/81** City of Toronto Archives, Globe and Mail Collection, Fonds 1266, Item 8177   **82** City of Toronto Archives, Fonds 1244, Item 1028M   **83** (upper) City of Toronto Archives, Globe and Mail Collection, Fonds 1266, Item 39776

83 (lower) City of Toronto Archives, Globe and Mail Collection, Fonds 1266, Item 8271   **84/85** City of Toronto Archives, Fonds 1244, Item 8045   **86** Toronto Public Library, Acc: 964-6-44a, Repro: T 31396   **87** City of Toronto Archives, Globe and Mail Collection, Fonds 1266, Item 5750   **88** City of Toronto Archives, Series 372, Sub-series 72, Item 1002   **89** Archives of Ontario, RG 9-7-5-0-59   **90** Archives of Ontario, RG 2-71, VA-5   **91** City of Toronto Archives, Fonds 1244, Item 1160B   **92** (upper) City of Toronto Archives, Globe and Mail Collection, Fonds 1266, Item 9439   **92** (lower) City of Toronto Archives, Globe and Mail Collection, Fonds 1266, Item 9440   **93** Archives of Ontario, Acc: 9254 S14190   **94** City of Toronto Archives, Series 372, Sub-series 100, Item 109   **95** City of Toronto Archives, SC 488, Item 5253   **96** City of Toronto Archives, Fonds 1244, Item 1956   **97** City of Toronto Archives, Fonds 1005, Item 62   **98/99** City of Toronto Archives, Fonds 1005, Item 65   **100/101** City of Toronto Archives, Series 372, Sub-series 32, Item 672   **102** City of Toronto Archives, Globe and Mail Collection, Fonds 1266, Item 5561   **103** City of Toronto Archives, Fonds 1005, Item 64   **104** Archives of Ontario, F 10-2-3-17   **105** City of Toronto Archives, Fonds 1244, Item 1682   **106/107** City of Toronto Archives, Fonds 1266, Item 1499   **108** City of Toronto Archives, Fonds 1244, Item 8030   **109** City of Toronto Archives, Fonds 1244, Item 3031   **110/111** City of Toronto Archives, Fonds 1244, Item 1684   **112** City of Toronto Archives, Fonds 1244, Item 1683   **113** City of Toronto Archives, Globe and Mail Collection, Fonds 1266, Item 6361   **114/115** City of Toronto Archives, Globe and Mail Collection, Fonds 1266, Item 39963   **116/117** City of Toronto Archives, Globe and Mail Collection, Fonds 1266, Item 39964   **118/119** Toronto Public Library, Acc: X 65-64, Repro: T 11552, Slide MTL 1798   **120** Archives of Ontario, F 1075/H649   **121** City of Toronto Archives, Globe and Mail Collection, Fonds 1266,

Item 8245   **122** Toronto Public Library, Acc: X 65-189, Repro: T 13358, Slide MTL 1460 **123** City of Toronto Archives, Globe and Mail Collection, Fonds 1266, Item 8244 **124** City of Toronto Archives, Globe and Mail Collection, Fonds 1266, Item 9095 **125** Metro Toronto Reference Library, T30346   **126** Archives of Ontario, C 7-3, 19126B   **127** City of Toronto Archives, Fonds 1244, Item 8100   **128** Archives of Ontario, C 7-3, 20304   **129** City of Toronto Archives, Fonds 1266, Item 6845 **130/131** City of Toronto Archives, Fonds 1488, Item 1837   **132** City of Toronto Archives, Fonds 1266, Item 8020   **133** (upper) Archives of Ontario, F 1405-23-76, MSR 6692-4   **133** (lower) Archives of Ontario, F 1405-15-59, MSR 7382-1 **134** City of Toronto Archives, Fonds 1244, Item 8144   **135** Toronto Public Library, Acc: X 65-68, Repro: T 12909   **136** City of Toronto Archives, Fonds 1266, Item 7506 **137** City of Toronto Archives, Fonds 1244, Item 1940   **138** City of Toronto Archives, Series 372, Sub-series 32, Item 817 **139** City of Toronto Archives, SC 266, Item 1881   **140** National Archives Canada, Acc: 1971-120, John Boyd Collection, Item 18368A   **141** Archives of Ontario, C 57-1-2-153.1   **142/143** City of Toronto Archives, Series 71, Item 12453   **144** City of Toronto Archives, Globe and Mail Collection, Fonds 1266, Item 39434   **145** City of Toronto Archives, Globe and Mail Collection, Fonds 1266, Item 7738   **146** City of Toronto Archives, Globe and Mail Collection, Fonds 1266, Item 7252   **147** Archives of Ontario, RG 2-71/WX-1   **148/149** City of Toronto Archives, Fonds 1244, Item 8191   **150** City of Toronto Archives, Globe and Mail Collection, Fonds 1266, Item 8857 **151** City of Toronto Archives, Fonds 1244, Item 1842   **152** City of Toronto Archives, Fonds 1244, Item 8197   **153** Toronto Public Library, Acc: 986-5, Repro: T 31735 **154** City of Toronto Archives, Fonds 1244, Item 1619   **155** City of Toronto Archives, Fonds 1244, Item 4091   **156** City of Toronto Archives, Fonds 1244, Item 8130

157 City of Toronto Archives, Fonds 1244, Item 1608   **159** City of Toronto Archives, Fonds 1244, Item 1641   **160** Archives of Ontario, RG 2-71/COT-133   **161** City of Toronto Archives, Globe and Mail Collection, Fonds 1266, Item 2495 **162/163** City of Toronto Archives, Globe and Mail Collection, Fonds 1266, Item 8611 **164** City of Toronto Archives, Globe and Mail Collection, Fonds 1266, Item 5762 **165** City of Toronto Archives, Fonds 1244, Item 2019   **166/167** City of Toronto Archives, Globe and Mail Collection, Fonds 1266, Item 6127   **168/169** City of Toronto Archives, Fonds 1244, Item 2034   **170** City of Toronto Archives, Fonds 1244, Item 3033 **171** City of Toronto Archives, Fonds 1244, Item 1163   **172** City of Toronto Archives, Fonds 1244 Item 2033   **173** City of Toronto Archives, Globe and Mail Collection, Fonds 1266, Item 8697   **174/175** City of Toronto Archives, Fonds 1244, Item 2009 **176/177** City of Toronto Archives, Series 71, Item 3629   **178/179** City of Toronto Archives, Globe and Mail Collection, Fonds 1266, Item 39857   **180** City of Toronto Archives, Fonds 1244, Item 1096   **181** City of Toronto Archives, Fonds 1244, Item 1156 **182** City of Toronto Archives, Series 71, Item 4082   **183** City of Toronto Archives, Globe and Mail Collection, Fonds 1266, Item 5509   **184/185** City of Toronto Archives, Series 71, Item 5986   **186** (upper) Archives of Ontario, C 7-3, 20296B   **186** (lower) Archives of Ontario, C 7-3, 18922 **187** (upper) Archives of Ontario, C 7-3, 20228   **187** (lower) Archives of Ontario, C 57, 18189   **188** City of Toronto Archives, Fonds 1244, Item 1714   **189** Toronto Public Library, Acc: 979-38-2, Repro: T 10161   **190** City of Toronto Archives, Fonds 1244, Item 1024   **191** City of Toronto Archives, Globe and Mail Collection, Fonds 1266, Item 9984 **192** City of Toronto Archives, Globe and Mail Collection, Fonds 1266, Item 5706 **193** City of Toronto Archives, Globe and Mail Collection, Fonds 1266, Item 7299 **194** City of Toronto Archives, Globe and Mail Collection, Fonds 1266, Item 7744

195 City of Toronto Archives, Globe and Mail Collection, Fonds 1266, Item 39660 **196/197** City of Toronto Archives, Globe and Mail Collection, Fonds 1266, Item 39567   **198** City of Toronto Archives, Globe and Mail Collection, Fonds 1266, Item 39396   **199** City of Toronto Archives, Globe and Mail Collection, Fonds 1266, Item 1071 **200** City of Toronto Archives, Fonds 1244, Item 3040   **201** City of Toronto Archives, Fonds 1244, Item 3038   **202** City of Toronto Archives, Globe and Mail Collection, Fonds 1266, Item 39458 **203** City of Toronto Archives, Globe and Mail Collection, Fonds 1266, Item 39471 **205** Archives of Ontario, RG 10-30-2, 1.8.14(B)   **206/207** Archives of Ontario, RG 10-30-2, 1.8.9   **208** Archives of Ontario, RG 2-71, SHC-52   **209** Archives of Ontario, RG 2-71, SHC-26   **210** Archives of Ontario, F1075/H2012   **211** City of Toronto Archives, Globe and Mail Collection, Fonds 1266, Item 5820   **212** City of Toronto Archives, Globe and Mail Collection, Fonds 1266, Item 39445   **213** Toronto Public Library, Acc: X 65-55, Repro: T 12276 **214/215** Toronto Public Library, Acc: X 65-110, Repro: T 32374   **216** National Archives of Canada, Acc: 1971-271

Quotations

Sources for material appearing in quotation marks are cited below. Please see References for the complete citations of books.

27 Dendy and Kilbourn, *Toronto Observed,* p. 228. **54** As quoted in White, *Too Good To Be True,* p. 152. **88** As quoted in MacDougall, *Activists and Advocates,* p. 77. **95** As quoted in Lemon, *Toronto Since 1918,* p. 77. **118** Kluckner: *Toronto: The Way It Was,* p. 142. **204** As quoted in MacDougall, *Activists and Advocates,* p. 97. **213** Harney and Troper, *Immigrants: A Portrait of the Urban Experience, p.* v.

Index

l